R.I

Costume Reference 6

The Victorians

MARION SICHEL

B. T. Batsford London

First published 1978
Reprinted 1979
© Marion Sichel 1978

ISBN 0 7134 0344 6

Typeset by Tek-Art Ltd
Printed in Great Britain by
The Anchor Press Ltd and bound by
Wm Brendon & Son Ltd
both of Tiptree, Essex
for the publishers B.T. Batsford Ltd,
4 Fitzhardinge Street, London W1H 0AH

Contents

Under her straw bonnet the little girl has her hair parted in the centre with ringlets hanging at the sides. The ankle length dress reveals the pantelettes, and the dress overskirt is hitched up.

Introduction

With so much information about costume available during Victoria's reign (1837-1901) in the form of fashion plates, advertisements and, of course, photographs, it is important to try and identify some of the main strands of fashion history.

Although London had now firmly established itself as the centre of menswear, Paris still reigned supreme in female fashion. Ironically, though, it is an Englishman, Charles Frederick Worth, who is credited with the foundation in the 1830s of *Haute Couture* (an exclusive circle of dress designers) — a Parisian phenomenon which increased its power over women's fashion as the century progressed until it almost achieved the status of a religious cult!

Set against this idea of *exclusivity* is the ever increasing influence of mass manufacture and growth of *standardization* of clothes for the swelling numbers of the middle class. Men, particularly, were settling into the 'uniform' of the dark suit which is still so strong today. The suit, especially later in the century, seems to express some of the strongest Victorian values — 'modesty', 'conformity' and 'respectability' — above all 'responsibility' as against 'flashiness' and frivolity.

As Victoria's reign progressed the cult of the monarchy became stronger and stronger, and, of course, was strongly influential in costume. In the costume descriptions which follow the names of Victoria and her consort, Albert, crop up again and again attached to articles of clothing.

Women's clothes seem to express another side of Victorian

society, the love of decoration and 'richness' — ruching, frills, bows, bustles, rich colours and materials all made their contribution to female finery, seen at its height during the 'Crinoline period' of 1840-70. However, women were beginning to see their role differently as the century passed, and although there was no widespread questioning of the traditional female role until the early years of the twentieth century things were changing. Women, although not emancipated, were more *active*. Sports such as tennis, cycling, croquet, even golf, were played by women and clothes had to adapt to these new circumstances. Bustles were reduced or disappeared, corsets relaxed, skirts rose slightly, and a fresh sense of functionality moved through women's fashion. It is interesting, also, to see specifically male fashions being adapted and adopted by women: for example the naval reefer jacket or the French African 'zouave' jacket made famous during the Crimean War, as was the 'cardigan' and the 'raglan' sleeve (both named after British commanders).

It is in the Victorian period that we can see most clearly the seeds of the twentieth century, not least as it is expressed through fashion.

Victorian Men

TAIL COATS

Tail coats were single or double-breasted and worn as dress coats on formal occasions, day or evening, as well as for riding. Double-breasted coats usually had a button stand (a separate border of material attached to the main body of the front of the coat) for the buttons and buttonholes.

Coat tails reached the knees and were slightly rounded, the length from neck to waist being about equal to that from the waist to the base of the tails. The collar, which was low, could have a V- or M-notch and joined the large lapels. Both collar and cuffs were often trimmed with velvet with small and round or slit and closed cuffs with two buttons. Pockets were concealed in the pleats at the sides and for day wear the front could be closed with four buttons, whilst for evening wear the buttons were usually left undone.

From the 1840s the top of the left lapel could have an extra buttonhole to hold a flower, although until about 1865 the top buttonhole was often used for this purpose. In the 1850s tail coats were also known as 'dress' coats or 'swallow-tail' coats, with the waist at normal level and the tails slightly shorter than previously. After about 1885 the length from neck to waist became shorter whilst that from the waist to the end of the skirts became longer. When worn for full dress occasions sleeves and skirts were usually lined in satin or silk. They also had a deep roll collar and an M-notch and low lapels but after about 1855 the M-notch was only popular for evening wear. The sleeves, which were wide at the shoulders, narrowed towards the wrists and ended in closed cuffs. Pockets were at waist level and concealed by small flaps. For day wear the dress coat was cut back just beneath waist level with the tails cut square from the sides, reaching almost to knee level. Although the coat could be buttoned for day wear, this was rarely done for evening attire, although it could be fastened near the top with a *tibi* (button and loop). There were between four and five buttons down the front, depending on the length available.

By the end of the 1860s dress coats were worn mainly for evenings or livery. In the 1870s the dress coat, still worn for evening wear and mainly in black, had one of the button-holes in the lapel which originally pointed upwards, but was gradually squared with a small step. The coat was also square cut and the tails tapered towards the bottom. The narrow sleeves ended in cuffs which had two to three buttons. Pockets were again concealed in the pleats or seams.

Dandies of the 1830s known as 'Mashers' created a new fashionable style of dress coat. This appeared early in the 1880s and by the end of the decade was very popular. This type of dress coat, tight waisted and worn with stays, had a low roll collar merging with the lapels which were faced with corded silk. Cuffs were stitched and ended with one button. By the 1890s the silk-lined rolled collar and lapels in one reached as low as the two bottom buttons in the front, a collar with a step being worn mainly only by servants. However, about 1893 the step roll collar again became popular and shoulders became more squared and the skirts of the coat became longer. Cuffs had three buttons and the length of the coat from neck to waist was now equal to the length from there to the base of the tails. By about 1895 the skirts at the back became longer in proportion to the back from neck to waist. They also became more tapered and spoon shaped. The lapels came so low that only two buttons were necessary in the front and cuffs by this time had no buttons. It is a basic tail coat shape which has not altered to this day.

Known as a dinner jacket from about 1898, a dress lounge coat became popular about 1888. Worn informally for dinners, parties and theatres, it had a roll collar in one with the lapels which ended at waist level. There were just one or two buttons and buttonholes. The collar and lapels were faced in a silk material. The jacket, which could have side pockets, was never worn closed and the sleeves were similar to those of a dress coat.

Ulster coat with a cape and a half belt at the back, c. 1876.

8

FROCK COATS

From about 1840 side bodies came into general use. Until this period coats had been made with three seams: one centre back, and one on each side under the arms. To ensure a better fit, side pieces (about 10cm wide) were inserted under the armholes, thus making five seams and six pieces of material.

Frock coats were an important feature of a gentleman's attire. They could be either single or double-breasted, the double-breasted styles normally having a button stand. Generally long waisted with short skirts until about 1855 frock coat waists became longer and the skirts shorter.

Collars were buttoned fairly high if there were no lapels present. If there were lapels an M-notch (until the 1850s) or a V-notch were popular. The close-fitting sleeves were plain at the shoulders and ended either closed or slit at the wrists.

The *Taglioni* frock coat, popular from the 1830s, with a narrow collar and lapels and short, full skirts, now had side bodies and sometimes a Prussian collar which was a stand-fall type with ends almost meeting in the front.

The *surtout*, another name for frock coat, could be either single or double-breasted and was close fitting ending above the knees. The full skirts usually had rounded ends. For the single-breasted style the collar was usually a roll variety, merging into the lapels, whilst the double-breasted frock coat could have the collar notched with a wide lapel. The close-fitting sleeves ended with either a small cuff or a slit with a button at the wrists. Pockets were accommodated in the pleats, whilst a breast pocket was placed on the left for a handkerchief. This lasted until about 1877 when it became less popular.

By the 1850s the surtout was indistinguishable from the generally worn frock coats which were first worn on informal occasions but by about 1850 were also being worn as dress coats for formal wear. In the decade 1850-60 the waist became less obvious and the skirts hung straighter. About 1869 short frocks became fashionable with fairly small collars and lapels. Sleeves were peg topped, ending in a round cuff. In the 1860s the fit became looser with skirts not so full, giving the whole garment a straighter look.

In the 1870s double-breasted frock coats had four pairs of buttons whilst single-breasted styles had two. Tapering sleeves ended in sham cuffs and the collar, often of velvet,

Morning coat, c. 1880s.

The gentleman on the left is wearing a morning coat, single-breasted waistcoat with a shawl collar and straight trousers. Spats were also worn by both gentlemen. The little boy in the centre is dressed in a jacket and skirt with a blouse and large lace collar. Beneath the skirt are seen the frilled drawers that were so popular. The gentleman on the right wears a type of pilot coat, single-breasted, with checked trousers which were fashionable at this period, and both men are wearing toppers, one with a petersham band. 1850s.

Morning jacket with breast pocket worn over a single-breasted waistcoat, c. 1858.

ended with narrow lapels. The edges of the coat could be trimmed with braid. By about 1873 single-breasted frock coats were more fashionable, buttoning high up to conceal the waistcoat worn beneath.

At the start of the 1880s frock coats became less popular, morning coats taking their place, but by the 1890s the frock coat was again in fashion for a brief time, with a higher waist and longer skirts. The buttons which had been four in number were reduced to three, the silk-faced lapels became narrower and reached the top button, skirts became fuller and reached knee level. In this period double-breasted waistcoats were the correct attire to wear beneath frock coats, which were often left unbuttoned.

MORNING OR RIDING COATS

The riding coat was really another kind of tail coat with sloping fronts from the bottom button, instead of the straight horizontal line.

As riding took place mainly during the mornings this coat was also known as a morning coat and could be worn on informal occasions. As the coat became more fashionable it was worn for formal wear, gradually taking the place of the frock coat by the 1880s. The morning coat was similar in cut to the dress coat and even underwent the same alterations.

A riding or morning coat, also known as a 'Newmarket' or 'cut-away', could be either single or double-breasted and was worn open or with the top button fastened or closed by a tibi (see Glossary). The turned-down collars sometimes had no lapels to follow. Sleeves usually had slit cuffs whilst the waist was slightly longer than that of the dress or frock coat. There was a high roll collar and lapels with full sleeves ending at the wrists without cuffs. Another style called a 'Doncaster' riding coat was similar except that the coat was looser and the skirts fuller.

In the 1850s the morning coat still resembled a frock, but the fronts sloped away to form broad tails with the edges usually bound. It was generally single-breasted with pockets in the pleats or at the waistline with flaps. On the left there could be a breast pocket, and occasionally also a ticket pocket.

In the 1860s the morning coat was often called a 'shooting' coat and could be either single or double-breasted with the fronts less curved. Before the mid-1860s the longer waists necessitated five front buttons, whilst later, when the waists became shorter, only two or three buttons were required. When the waists became shorter, the curves again became more prominent, the fronts reaching to knee level, being either rounded or square cut. The collar was low with short lapels. However, in warm weather, the lapels were turned down low to the waist. There could also be a buttonhole to hold flowers at the turn of the lapel. Sleeves, which were peg topped, became more close fitting towards the 1870s as indeed was fashionable for all coats.

By the 1870s morning coats, also worn on horseback, replaced the Newmarket and riding coats. They had pockets hidden by flaps at the waist and low velvet collars. The edging of the coat could be bound or corded. The single-breasted morning coat had plain square skirts with three front buttons, but only one being closed. As the waist was lowered, the single-breasted style became more popular, often being worn instead of a frock coat. It was generally worn with a double-breasted fancy waistcoat.

About 1870 a variation, known as the 'University' coat, had the fronts in a long curve from the second button so that more of the waistcoat was seen. The base was cut at a more obtuse angle instead of having the corners rounded. Due to the difficulty in making this style double-breasted it was nearly always made in the single-breasted style with two front buttons. In the 1880s it merged in with the normal morning coat.

The single-breasted morning coat usually had three or four covered buttons. By about 1884 the waist was lower (about 5cm beneath the natural waistline) and the skirts were shortened often with braided edges. The plain unpadded sleeves ended in a stitched-down cuff with two buttons. Side pockets were in the pleats with the breast pocket on the left. About 1888 a pocket on the inside was also added, and by 1890 there were only three front buttons, the fronts usually being left undone. The silk-faced rolled lapels became narrower and reached the top button. After about 1895 the tails became slightly shorter and by about 1896 the waist again became higher with the longer tails reaching the knees. After about 1897 the outside breast pocket became less popular; lapels became straighter and more pointed and could have the edges in braid. The silk facing reached only to the buttons and buttonholes. The morning coat was extremely popular at the end of the century with the fronts cut away to make them quite narrow.

Chesterfield coat, c. 1876.

For informal wear lounge jackets were usually worn with matching waistcoats and trousers. They were made quite simply with the side seams having a dart from under the arms slightly forwards to the waist, thus making them fit better than the simple coat or paletot (see Glossary) of the previous period. The jackets, mainly single-breasted, had short skirts just covering the seat. They could have a seam at the waist and side pleats, and hip buttons, but more often than not no back vents. The fronts were slightly curved. If no seam was present at the waist, side pleats and hip buttons were absent, although a small vent at the back was possible. The fronts on this style were straight. The collar and lapels were fairly small, and pockets were on either side at about waist level. A handkerchief pocket on the left was customary. Sleeves were straight but became more peg topped in shape and without cuffs around 1858. From about 1853 the jacket was in the same material as the trousers, whilst the waistcoat could be of another material.

In about the same period — 1858 — a 'Tweedside' lounge jacket which came from Scotland was single-breasted and buttoned high at the neck with usually only the top three or four buttons closed. The collar was not large and the lapels were short. The pockets were mainly of the patch variety. The jacket was loose fitting without a central seam at the back. By about 1864 the Tweedside was cut longer and although fashionable was one of the most tasteless styles of dress.

About 1861 the fit of the jacket was improved with the insertion of side bodies. It then became known as the 'Oxonian' or 'jumper' (a short, straight coat with narrow collar, high buttoned, unlined and therefore mainly worn in summer), and could be either single or double-breasted with the fronts cut straight. The 'Cambridge', a style which came in in the 1870s, formed a slight curve, opening out to reveal the waistcoat. This became the more popular of the two styles, although the Oxonian was also worn. In the 1860s lounge jackets with only side seams and a central back seam were known as 'three-seamers'. These could have a back vent.

A double-breasted style of lounge jacket known as a 'reefer' or 'pea-jacket' became fashionable about 1865 and was short with a low collar and short lapels. Although there was no central back seam, there were short vents in the side

Double-breasted reefer jacket, c. 1885.

seams. Pockets could either be flapped or patch type as well as welted. A handkerchief pocket on the left breast and an inside right-hand pocket were quite usual. The double-breasted jacket had four pairs of buttons and the edges were either bound or braided. The reefer could also be worn in winter as an overcoat. By the 1870s it became less popular, although about 1878 a single-breasted version became fashionable with the younger generation. In the 1880s the single-breasted reefer and the Cambridge became indistinguishable, with a short roll collar buttoning high with four buttons and three seams. The fronts were straight with squared corners. The double-breasted reefer had squared lapels and vents were in the side seams. By the end of the 1880s reefers had lost their popularity as coats began to be worn more open.

In the 1860s the 'Prince of Wales' jacket (a looser version of the reefer with three pairs instead of four pairs of buttons) was also worn. It could be with or without a back seam and vents. The pockets could be braided at the edge or four flapped patch pockets could be present. Also in the same period, a lounge jacket popular in the country and worn buttoned high to the neck was called a 'Norfolk' and had a box pleat centre back as well as two box pleats in the front. The collar (front opening) and the base of the sleeves were finished like a shirt with an edging. There were two flapped pockets and around the waist was a belt of the same material as the jacket. This type of jacket was often worn with knickerbockers and a deerstalker hat. From the 1880s Norfolk jackets became increasingly fashionable and could be worn with bowlers. About 1894 they were often yoked with the box pleats emerging from the yoke and this, by the end of the century, established itself as the general design of the Norfolk jacket.

In the 1880s single-breasted lounge jackets had rounded corners, four outside pockets, including a ticket pocket. The jackets were made with three seams, with the side seams sometimes reaching the top of the side pockets. The jacket reached the bottom of the trouser seat. Sleeves when short enough revealed the fashionable linen shirt cuffs and ended with cuffs formed by double stitching and three buttons and buttonholes. The jacket was buttoned with four or five buttons. In the 1890s lounge jackets were left more open and about 1895 only three buttons were considered fashionable. Also, it became general to have no central seam

Norfolk jacket, c. 1888.

Double-breasted reefer, c. 1885.

Golf costume jacket.

Bicycling costume, c. 1888.

at the back. By about 1898 the lounge jacket was the most popular form of jacket and also became known as the 'dinner' jacket.

WAISTCOATS

Sleeved waistcoats which had previously been worn came back into fashion in the form of knitted cardigans. If they had collars these were usually of either velvet or of the rolled variety.

Single- or double-breasted waistcoats were usually waist-length with or without collars and revers, slightly pointed in the front until the 1850s when they became straight. In the early 1850s waistcoats could match the trousers and by the early 1870s they often matched both jackets and trousers.

For formal and evening wear they were more ornate and made in contrasting colours, white or black being worn in the evenings. For day wear waistcoats tended to be single breasted with rolled lapels, sometimes wide enough to fold over a coat. There were about eight buttons, usually covered in the same cloth as the waistcoat material, with the bottom button about 1cm from the base. There could be two to three pockets, the third being a watch pocket and placed higher.

Waistcoats were often corded at the edges with the fronts at the base often leather lined, the backs of the waistcoats being of a cheaper material and with a short vent. To give a better fit a strap and buckle were used, although tapes were still in use at the back.

By the 1840s waistcoats were always double-breasted for evening wear. They were made of materials such as velvets or satins with embroidered designs and lined in silk. They could have small stepped or rolled collars and six buttons of self-material or precious stones. For day wear single-breasted waistcoats often had the flat collar and lapels in a different material from the fronts. The edges could be either stitched or bound. By the 1850s there were usually six buttons ending higher than previously. The two pockets had welts and a watch was often carried in one of them with the chain passing through a buttonhole. From about 1853 double-breasted styles became popular for morning wear and also when worn with a single-breasted frock coat. (Double-breasted frock coats were worn with single-breasted waist-coats.) The lapels were wider and could be pointed, with the points buttoned back; fastening was with three or four pairs of buttons. When worn with lounge suits the single-breasted waistcoat could have a narrow turnover collar and short stepped lapels, or it could be collarless. When frock coats were worn the double-breasted version usually had a roll collar.

In the 1850s, single-breasted waistcoats with shawl collars forming a V-opening or a rolled collar and narrow lapels (often in a different colour) were also popular. The four to six buttons could also be of cut steel as well as the usual covered or stone ones. Braid decoration became more usual than embroidery. From the 1870s the long wide V-shaped opening was formed by the lapels and turned collar reaching the point where the waistcoat was buttoned with its two to three buttons. About 1873 the waistcoat could be double breasted with two pairs of buttons. By about 1884 the opening became wider, resembling a horseshoe shape ending with three or four buttons. The roll collar could be trimmed with either braid or faced with silk.

When the dinner jacket first came into vogue in the 1880s, it was worn with a white waistcoat with five buttons. The back of the waistcoat was tightened with straps and buckles.

By the 1890s the horseshoe-fronted waistcoat did not always have collar and lapels, but the fronts were edged in russia braid, and ended with three buttons. About 1888 waistcoats began to match the frocks and morning coats although trousers could still be of a different material. Before that date materials were checked or striped as well as having elaborate designs.

In the 1890s there were several fashionable styles such as the 'Goff' vest (a single-breasted and collarless type edged with braid and made of wool); the 'Newmarket' and 'Tattershall' were again collarless and of a checked material. A very ornate style known as the 'Willow' was worn towards the end of the century. This was of a material with a traditional Chinese blue willow-pattern design.

When worn with lounge suits, waistcoats usually had four pockets and, from about 1895, a special hole for the watch chain to pass through was also introduced. Darts in the front also helped to give the waistcoat a better fit as well as the back being tightened with a strap and buckle. Sometimes the strap was even made of elastic.

Plain cloth waistcoat edged in braid, 1850s.

Waistcoat with narrow lapels, 1870s.

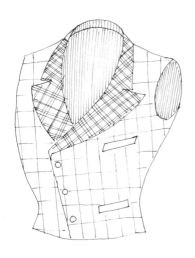

Wide lapelled waistcoat, 1870s.

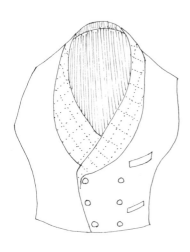

Waistcoat with roll collar, 1870s.

LEGWEAR

Breeches which remained similar to those of the earlier period, with the front closure of flap or fall, were now worn mainly only for sport, country wear or for ceremonial occasions.

Pantaloons were generally made of a stretch material sewn on to a waistband with a vent and puff at the back to ensure a better fit. The front opening was either with a small fall or a fly. There were also brace buttons at the waist. Pantaloons were tight fitting and were strapped under the foot to keep them taut. The slits at the ankles were closed by buttons which could be hidden by a fly or they were tied with ribbon. In the 1840s pantaloons were worn for walking out but by the 1850s were worn mainly only for riding and hunting.

Trousers were generally narrow in cut and made with only slight variations. They were worn with straps under the instep until the middle of the century. They could be cut straight all the way down or cut with gaiter bottoms, i.e. the side seams brought slightly forward. There was also a looser form of trouser, similar to the 'cossacks' of the early 1800s, which were loose from the waist, being gathered on to a waistband, becoming narrower further down. About 1857 an American style became popular in England. It was gathered on to a band at the waist with side pockets in the seams and could be worn without braces, as the back could be tightened with a buckle and strap. Also, at the same time, a peg-topped style made its appearance. The legs were wide around the hips, tightening at the ankles, matching, in fact, the type of sleeves so popular in this period. By the 1850s stripes and checks were very popular as well as a narrow band of different coloured material sewn down on the outside seam. By the 1870s nearly all trousers had a fly front and were without a waistband and from about 1876 the legs were tight to the knees and then flared out slightly. These trousers were popularly worn with reefer jackets. Cross pockets, pockets placed horizontally, became more fashionable than the side ones. Trousers throughout the years varied slightly in width. By the 1890s, however, the bottoms could be turned up, and a trouser press was used to give a firm crease line down the front. A hip pocket was also introduced as well as the two side pockets.

The 'Mashers' of the 1880s wore trousers very tight (also known as 'slacks') to the knees, becoming wide at the bottom. The trousers were so cut as to reveal the patent leather buttoned boots.

Knickerbockers (a new form of loose breeches) began to be worn in the 1860s. They originated from the uniform of the Rifle Volunteers and were mainly worn for walking and sport. Made loose and baggy they had a wide knee band that could either be buttoned or fastened with a buckle and strap which was often hidden by the fullness of the material above it. By about 1869 knickerbockers were of the same materials as Norfolk jackets (tweed being most popular) with which they were very often worn. Knickerbockers became increasingly popular as the century progressed.

Braces were worn buttoned with bone or metal buttons on each side of the front and one each side of the vent at the back of the trousers. But by about 1850, when the back vent was no longer much in use, buttons were sewn on to two slightly raised points either side of the back seam. There were now often two buttons each side at the back, so that braces had two bands which were joined forming two V-shapes. The two front parts were, ideally, half the front waist measurement apart. Braces were often embroidered and by the 1860s the fronts had double sliding ends, so that they were adjustable to the length required.

Loose cross-over collar style for young boy, c. 1840.

NECKWEAR

In the 1840s there were several styles of *cravats*, the most traditional being a large bow with pointed ends. There were diverse styles that included the 'Joinville' which had square ends either fringed or lace edged. It was such a large cravat that it protruded beyond the width of the neck. This type of cravat was made fashionable by the Prince of Joinville. The 'Byron' was a very narrow, shoe-string like piece of material and was usually worn with the collar turned over. Large cravats were usually worn with ornamental tie pins. From the early 1860s until the 1890s when coats were usually buttoned high, very little neckwear was seen, but in the 1890s the variety of neckwear became much greater.

Stocks or shaped bands were worn and were tied or buckled at the back. They were worn mainly with sports clothes, and gradually went out of fashion. A *scarf*, previously known as a kerchief, was also worn. This covered the front of the shirt and was fastened with a tiepin. One style known, rather confusingly, as the Joinville, bore no resemblance to the earlier Joinville cravat of the 1840s and became fashionable about 1895. This style came from America and was worn with a scarf ring.

Open-necked shirt style for young boy, c. 1847.

Gentleman with Dundreary whiskers wearing a full flat bow tie, c. 1857.

Gentleman wearing a butterfly collar with a necktie with a large knot, and having a short hairstyle, c. 1895.

In the 1890s various *neckties* became very popular. They had a variety of names such as the bow tie which was in a butterfly or batswing shape. A very narrow piece of material could also be worn; this was like a shoe lace and known as a 'string tie'. A 'four-in-hand' or 'Derby' became very fashionable about 1894. This was a tie with a knot at the neck and the ends hanging down one over the other, the ends very often being squared. From the mid-1890s ties were made in a large selection of materials such as corduroy, silks and satins. About 1897 the mode for willow patterns was strong. Sometimes ties were sold ready-made, that is they were already tied in the correct manner and were just worn around the neck and fastened from behind. For evening attire a butterfly bow of a white material such as piqué was usually worn.

Collars were originally attached to shirts and were deep enough to be turned over a cravat or stock. From the 1850s a separate starched collar was worn and by the 1890s rose to about 8cm. One of the first separate collars was of the stand-up variety known as the 'Piccadilly'. Another similar style was the 'Dux' which had the points in the front turned down. The 'Shakespere' was a stand-fall style with the points being quite large. A plain stand collar, also known as a dog collar, had the fronts almost meeting.

OUTDOOR WEAR

Overcoats or top coats were made under a variety of different names. In the 1840s the 'Chesterfield' (named after the sixth earl, a notable leader of fashion), single or double-breasted, had no waist or back seam, but it was slightly shaped. It had a short vent at the back but was without side pleats. The Chesterfield reached the knees, but by the 1870s became shorter. In the 1850s the coat, single or double-breasted, was not very shaped and was still without a waist seam, but a seam at the back ended with a vent. There were still no side pleats or hip buttons. Pockets were concealed by flaps, or they could be just slit. A small ticket pocket was made just above the right hand pocket from about 1859. A left breast pocket also became popular. After about 1858 peg-topped sleeves became fashionable. The Chesterfield was one of the most fashionable of coats. It was closed with between four to five buttons covered in the same material as the coat and hidden by a fly front. The collar was of the turn-over type in velvet with silk

The lady is wearing a winter style coat with 'kick-up' sleeves and a hat decorated with plumes, c. 1896. The gentleman is wearing a fur lined and trimmed pelisse and a top hat, c. 1872.

Gentleman wearing round-crown felt bowler hat, a knee length, single-breasted overcoat with a flapped breast pocket and a velvet collar, c. 1895.

facings and narrow notched lapels. Cross pockets with braided edges were just below the waistline. Sometimes there was also a breast pocket on the left. In the 1870s the sleeves were for a short while peg topped again, but then became closer fitting with cuffs and buttons. By about 1875 the coat became longer, ending about 8cm below knee level and by about 1878 it became even longer, reaching the calves. The edges of the coat could be bound with braid. There were four to five buttons to the waist only, which could be hidden by a fly.

In the early 1880s the Chesterfield again became shorter and close fitting. The base of the side seams could have vents. About 1885 the coat often had a detachable shoulder cape to elbow length. It was sewn on to a band at the neck edge and could be buttoned to the collar. About 1889 the coat again became longer and looser and the sleeves became fuller. The collar, as always, was of velvet and faced with silk.

In the 1890s the Chesterfield, still the most elegant of coats, was mainly single-breasted and made in three main styles. The long style, reaching calf length, was at its longest about 1895 and was slightly shaped with a back seam and a short vent with the pockets placed at a slant. The 'sac back' Chesterfield reached the knees and had short side vents, but no seam at the back. About 1890 the Chesterfield style had a cape to elbow length and no sleeves, just wide armholes which were covered by the cape.

The *paletot* (the French name for an overcoat originally called a *pardessus*), or 'pilot coat', was a short-waisted great coat resembling a top frock coat and could be worn without a jacket beneath. The paletot seldom had a seam at the waist, and if there was one present it would only be in the front, beneath waist level, the skirts being one with the forefront. There was seldom a back vent and there were no pleats in the side seams. The buttons in front were often concealed by a fly. Two variations of this coat were the 'paletot sac', single-breasted with a hood instead of a collar and a double-breasted paletot sac which was loose fitting and similar to the Chesterfield. By the end of the 1870s the name paletot ceased to be used.

From about 1892 a summer overcoat known as the 'paddock' was made with side bodies in the underarm seams. There were no back or waist seams. The skirts were full and deep side pleats covered a back vent with a large

Gentleman wearing a double-breasted frock coat with a short waist and long skirts with silk faced lapels, c. 1897.

21

overlap. The flapped pockets included two side, one breast and one ticket pocket, whilst there was sometimes another pocket on the inside. This was a longer and smarter version of the Chesterfield and with the 'Ascot', a similar style, was worn mainly by sporting gentlemen.

In the 1840s the 'curricle' coat, formerly known as a 'box' coat (other names were Taglioni overcoat and top frock coat), had one or more capes. It was fitted and had a waist similar in cut to a frock coat; it was often double breasted with a velvet collar. The frock coat varied in length, about mid-thigh until about 1854 when skirts almost reached down to the ankles and then again were shortened to the knees. In the 1860s another name, the 'Albert' top frock, was similar in style with a short waist and long skirts and flapped pockets at the waist seam. The collar was also deep, almost cape-like, lying flat to the shoulders and made of either velvet or sealskin. About 1893 the Albert top frock was double-breasted and close fitting all the way down and had no connection with the Albert overcoat of the 1870s.

In the 1870s the top frock overcoat had wide lapels and cuffs. The collar was usually of velvet. Closure was with three or four buttons and in the early 1870s the single-breasted style was favoured, whereas later double-breasted styles became more popular. In about 1895 the coat was almost ankle length again with pockets under flaps at the waist. The edges of the coat could be either corded or piped. In the 1850s the 'Tweedside' overcoat was made similar to the jacket of that name, but reached the knees. It also had patch pockets.

A 'wrapper' was a loose thigh-length coat, not often closed with buttons, but more usually wrapped over and held closed by hand. The deep shawl collar was faced with silk or velvet, and the sleeves were close fitting. This type of coat was popular over evening dress.

The 'Ulster', an ankle-length overcoat, appeared about 1869 and had a detachable hood and, as it had a belt, was also known as a 'belted sac'. The Ulster became quite popular in the 1870s and could be single-breasted but was more often double-breasted. Sometimes the belt was just a piece at the back attached in the side seams. It often had a removeable hood or cape and stand collar buttoned beneath the attached turned-down collar of the coat itself. About 1875 a ticket pocket was introduced in the wrist part of the left sleeve. By the 1890s it was usual for the Ulster to have just a half

Ulster coat with a detachable cape, c. 1880.

The lady is in a pelerine-mantlet edged with lace frilling worn over a carriage dress, c. 1844. The gentleman is wearing a double-breasted Chesterfield with the sleeves full at the shoulders, narrowing towards the cuffs.

belt at the back. The double-breasted style usually had very large horn or pearl buttons, whilst the single-breasted version was normally fastened by a fly.

An 'Albert' overcoat of the 1870s (not to be confused with the Albert frock overcoat), had a fly front fastening with a semi-circular cape, a deep back vent and vertical slit pockets on each side above the waist, and flapped pockets at hip level. The coat reached to about the calves.

In the 1870s a short double-breasted overcoat with a shoulder cape and trimmed with astrakhan was named after the then Prime Minister, Gladstone.

In the 1880s a 'covert' (also known as a 'cover' coat) was like a short fly-fronted Chesterfield. It had no back seam and the vents were in the side seams. It was worn mainly for riding. By about 1897 the sleeves were of the raglan type (named after Lord Raglan of Crimean War fame) and the coat was then known as a 'Raglan covert'.

A 'Raglan' overcoat of about 1898 was a revival of the poncho. The back of the coat was cut on the cross; the side seams had a vent with two holes and could be buttoned. The coat was closed by a fly front, and the pockets were vertical. This coat, reaching almost to the ankles, was usually made in a waterproof material and gradually replaced the mackintosh which had been popular since the 1820s. The vents in the side seams of the Raglan were so placed that it was both possible and permissible for the first time to walk with the hands in the trouser pockets.

Short summer overcoats were known as 'dusters'.

CAPES AND CLOAKS

Cloaks in the 1840s usually reached the knees and had small turned-down collars. Some had capes attached and even had sleeves. In the 1850s the 'Talma' cloak, knee length and sleeveless, had a turned-down collar and was worn mainly for evening wear. Sleeved cloaks became more popular in the 1850s with wide sleeves and a short full body. There were several styles — the 'poncho' had very wide pagoda-like sleeve, whilst the 'cape-paletot', known from about 1857 as the 'Inverness', had sleeves not quite so wide, and also had a cape. In the 1860s the Inverness cape was like a loose overcoat, knee length with the cape coming from a fitted collar. Sometimes there were large pockets in the front skirts. By the 1870s the cape of the Inverness was not completely loose, as it was caught into the seams at the sides

Long, loose Inverness cape with a deep cape emanating from a fitted collar, 1880s.

Back view of a knee-length covert coat with raglan sleeves and a close-fitting collar, and a cloth cap, c. 1899.

24

1 *The young lady* on the left wears a morning dress with close-fitting jacket bodice with short basques attached. The ruched silk bonnet has a bavolet and ribbon decoration. *The boy* in the foreground is wearing a sailor suit and hat, the loose trousers being buttoned to the blouse. *The lady* on the right has a close-fitting bodice ending in a point, and the full gathered skirt is decorated with flounces of the same material. The square shawl, folded diagonally, is edged with a fringing. *The gentleman* in the background is wearing a paletot jacket and holding a silk top hat. *c.*1848.

2 *The gentleman* in the background has a fur-trimmed pilot coat over a frock coat which has velvet-faced lapels. He is wearing spats over his shoes. *The young girl* is wearing a low-crowned straw 'boater' with a large bow decoration in the front. The dress is of the sailor type worn with a fill in, and the boots are high and laced up the front. *The lady* standing next to the child is wearing a dress with gigot sleeves, a gored skirt with the hem stiffened, and the bolero-type jacket is made in matching colour and decoration. The jabot at the neck is edged with lace. *The lady* on the extreme right has a dress with a low décolletage which reveals a high-necked chemisette. The small gigot sleeves continue to a point over the back of the hands. The skirt is of the umbrella shape and is trimmed similarly to the sleeves with black. *c.* 1895–1898.

Evening dress suit with a continuous roll collar to waist level. The coat was worn open, c. 1894.

Single-breasted morning coat, the tails reaching the back of the knees, c. 1894.

by the sleeves, sometimes known as Dolman cape sleeves. Mashers and dandies wore a variation of this called a 'Masher dust wrap' with evening attire. This style was also made with an incomplete cape with large armholes and wings, similar to the Dolman or Inverness cape.

By the 1890s the Inverness was made more close fitting. The cape ended just behind the arms, the front being closed by a fly front. There was no cape at the back. These wing-like parts were usually lined in silk and took the place of sleeves. Inside these wings a strip of material was sewn across so that the arm could rest on it and armholes were made large enough to enable the hands to reach down to the trouser pockets.

The 'Raglan' cape with sleeves of that name was like a loose overcoat. The sleeves did not fit into armholes. Instead they came to a point at the top of the neck edge where they were joined to the front and back of the garment at the collar seam.

A semi-circular cut cloak in the Spanish style was fastened at the neck and was usually just draped over one shoulder.

The 'paletot' cloak, not to be confused with the cape, was a short cloak with just slits for the arms to protrude.

FORMAL WEAR

For evening wear a double-breasted dress coat was usually worn, often of a dark colour and worn with a single-breasted waistcoat which was either silk or velvet and embroidered down the side in the front or in scroll patterns; an under-waistcoat of a different colour could also be worn. In the 1840s pantaloons were worn with evening attire and were short enough to reveal the stockings. Black trousers were also permitted.

By the 1850s waistcoats were mainly black or white with the edges decorated. In the 1860s tight black trousers were the mode. Instead of side pockets they had a cash pocket which was a semi-circular opening in the front. About 1880 the dress waistcoat went out of fashion and a red or black silk sash was worn around the waist. Plain bow ties in black were worn for evening wear, except for balls, when white was the common colour. Boots or pumps in black were worn with either a bow or buckle fastening. Patent-leather boots which could have suede tops were worn from the 1880s. 'Opera' or 'gibus' (see Glossary) hats were carried.

For *court* wear a single-breasted tail coat was worn in the

25

1840s with a stand-up collar. The pocket flaps, collar and cuffs could be gold decorated. Gold colour buttons were also worn on the white waistcoats. White breeches matched the rest of the outfit with gold embroidery and buttons. Lace frilled shirts were also popular, as were white stockings. Shoes also had gold buckles. In the 1860s dark colours were fashionable for single-breasted dress coats. The waistcoats were without collars and the trousers could have a stripe down the outer seam.

Mourning dress consisted of an all black outfit which included frock coat, waistcoat, trousers, necktie, gloves, stockings and shoes as well as a black hatband and even a black handkerchief. This was very modish in the 1870s.

From the 1840s the fashionable colour for *weddings* was blue. The dress coat could have a velvet collar. Under the dress coat two waistcoats were worn, the under-waistcoat in a plain satin with a roll collar, whilst the outer waistcoat, also of satin or damask, could be heavily embroidered. Black pantaloons were popular in this period. In the 1870s a dress frock coat or morning coat were both equally fashionable for weddings, although the morning coat was gaining in favour. This outfit was worn with light coloured trousers.

In the late 1890s a single-breasted lounge or morning coat with a waistcoat were the correct attire for *morning wear*. A bowler hat with a lounge suit and a silk hat with a morning coat was usual. Coloured shirts with white collars could be worn. For *receptions* silk lined and faced frock coats with matching waistcoats were worn with striped trousers. White shirts had high collars and could be worn with satin scarves. Silk hats were the usual mode, and patent leather boots were also popular.

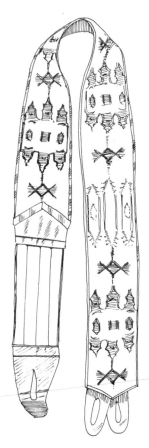

Embroidered brace, 1850s.

INFORMAL AND SPORTS WEAR

Dressing gowns worn in the morning and evening could be of satin with a large shawl collar and fastened around the waist with a girdle often with tasselled ends. Dressing gowns could be of satin or chintz, or any embroidered materials. Dressing gowns were often worn with a round nightcap.

Smoking jackets, worn from the 1850s, were often worn with a tasselled pork pie shaped cap. The jackets were generally fairly short, and made of various materials, but mainly velvets or quilted satins. They could be edged with cord and had roll collars. Fastening was generally by buttons and loops.

Types of collars.

The lady's dress has a pleated
lace yoke and upper part of the
sleeves, and the high neck is
covered with a jabot; the decoration is of silk braid. The gentleman is wearing a sporting cap
and yoked shooting jacket with
breeches, knitted stockings and
boots. Both c. 1897.

The gentleman is wearing a
boater of straw and a type of
blazer with straight trousers and
turn-ups. The lady is wearing a
high necked chemisette under a
jacket which matches her trained
skirt. c. 1896. She is also holding
a parasol.

In the 1840s a dress coat or Newmarket (riding coat) with trousers and waistcoat were worn with half boots and spurs as well as a top hat for *riding.* By the 1870s a single-breasted lounge jacket and checked waistcoat with a vent could be worn. Short frock coats were also the mode. Corduroy breeches were popular for a short while. From the 1880s fashionable gentlemen who rode wore morning coats and riding breeches which were close fitting from the knees, the outside being closed by buttons. The inside of the legs were often faced with leather.

For *hunting* long boots were worn with scarlet coats of the frock or Newmarket style. The buttons often had hunting motifs embossed on them. The waistcoats were also often embroidered with hunting decorations such as foxes' heads. Top hats and jockey caps were the usual headwear.

For *shooting*, jackets were generally of a waterproof material and had many pockets; trousers were fairly tight and buttoned at the base. Often waterproof ones were worn over ordinary trousers. By the 1870s knickerbockers were popular and later, in the 1890s, Norfolk jackets were also worn. Broad-brimmed hats, sometimes made of straw, were popular headwear.

Pea jackets, or 'monkey' jackets as they were sometimes known, as well as reefers, were worn with knickerbockers for *yachting.* Sailor or peaked hats were the mode and white canvas shoes were usual. For *cricket* short jackets and white trousers were worn in the 1870s. Blazers became the correct attire for both cricket and *tennis* from about 1887. The *football* outfit consisted of a striped jersey and stockings and knickerbockers. For *cycling* lounge jackets and breeches that buttoned at the knees were worn with striped stockings and high-buttoned boots. Peaked caps were also fashionable. *Golf* attire consisted of a morning coat or Norfolk jacket with either knickerbockers or trousers. Boots were laced and leather gloves were worn. Until about 1899 a golf cap could also be worn. This cap was also sometimes worn for cycling, as gentlemen often cycled to the golf course. The mode for *motoring* included a loose type of Chesterfield coat known either as a 'sac' or 'Albert driving cape'. Pantaloons were very fashionable.

FOOTWEAR

Shoes were often laced; the Oxonian shoes were laced through three to four eyelet holes with the vamp coming high up.

For evening wear pumps with buckles became fashionable, although ribbon ties were still worn.

Overshoes, such as galoshes and clogs, were worn throughout the remainder of the century. About 1844 rubber galoshes were worn by both men and women and were made in such a way so as to fit over shoes. Occasionally they were made so that the heel of the shoe protruded.

Elastic-sided boots became popular in the 1840s with an insertion of elastic possible on both sides. This type of boot was popular until the end of the century. High boots were only worn for riding and were known as 'top' boots or 'jockey' boots. 'Hessians', in the early 1860s, and 'Wellingtons', both high boots, were worn with pantaloons, but for evening wear Wellingtons, which had been fashionable, ceased to be worn. 'Highlows', a stronger pair of half boots, were laced up the front with six holes and were used mainly for country wear.

Gaiters which reached the knees were also known as 'spatterdashes'. Short gaiters or spats were worn with trousers; they were a type of spatterdash that buttoned on the outside with a strap passing under the shoe. Often spats were made of a canvas cloth in either grey or fawn.

Coloured and striped stockings were worn both in the daytime and for evening wear. Ribbed stockings were usually worn with knickerbockers as well as leggings.

Although lacing through eyelet holes was still in use in the 1860s, a new method of eyelet hooks and studs was introduced. Laces were criss-crossed over the metal hooks and tied at the top.

Hairstyle of the period, c. 1850.

Hairstyle of c. 1852.

Side parted hair and Imperial beard with short moustache. c. 1847.

Side parting with curled hair. c. 1849.

Slightly waved hair, moustache and goatee beard. c. 1850.

Hairstyle of c. 1852.

By the late 1870s Wellington boots had disappeared from fashion whilst button boots were more fashionable. Short evening boots were usually of patent leather whilst for country wear half boots which laced up the front and were known as 'Balmorals' were worn. Patent leather shoes were laced up the front. In the 1880s patent leather or suede boots that were buttoned were worn in the daytime, whilst for evening wear black pumps were essential.

In the 1890s shoes and boots became pointed except when worn for sport. Brown was the usual colour for footwear worn for sports, whilst for town wear black was the fashionable colour, but towards the end of the century russet was permissible for lounge wear.

HAIRSTYLES

Dandies not only led fashion in dress, but also often in hairstyles, just as the Macaronis had done in the eighteenth century.

In the 1840s hair became slightly longer and was curled with the back hair being combed forward. Another popular style was to wear smooth hair with the ends curled under at the back.

In the 1850s whiskers and beards became more popular and the Crimean War created the fashion for beards. The Imperial beard, a French import, was a slightly pointed beard, and a style fashionable among the Dandies. The Vandyke type of beard was also still worn. A goatee was a small chin beard which also became popular in the 1850s. 'Piccadilly weepers' or 'Dundreary whiskers', named after Lord Dundreary, a character in *Our American Cousin* by Tom Taylor, were very fashionable. They were long, pendant side whiskers and could be worn with beards or a drooping moustache.

Two main hairstyles were popular until the 1860s: the hair either waved or curled with usually a side parting (although the hair could be brushed straight back) or slightly longer and waved with a centre parting, the crown being worn flat and the sides brushed outwards. After the 1860s whiskers became smaller, but by the end of the century cavalry moustaches were in fashion.

Perfumed hair oil, imported and known as 'macassar', was used to keep the hair sleek. This began the fashion for the use of anti-macassars on the backs of chairs and settees, as this oil stained the materials.

Hair brushed straight back, c. 1855.

In the 1870s it was not usual to be clean shaven, bushy beards being the mode as well as any combination of moustache and whiskers. Hair again became shorter but still with a centre parting. From about 1880 hair was generally brushed straight back slightly raised in a Pompadour. Side whiskers became shorter and then lost popularity. Droopy moustaches became more popular whilst it was mainly older men who also wore beards. At the end of the century hair began to be worn with a side parting instead of the long fashionable centre parting, and hair also became shorter. Longer hair was considered artistic and was only worn by musicians and artists.

HEADWEAR

In the 1840s tall hats were generally the most popular. The crown usually curved out a little towards the top and the brims curled slightly at the sides. Top hats (stiff and finished in silk) for dress occasions were very tall until about 1865 after which they were reduced in height, but by the mid-1870s they had again become taller. They were also worn with frock coats, morning coats and dress coats. By the 1880s the shape became slightly bell-shaped and they had a curled brim. By the end of Victoria's reign the top hat had lost its popularity.

Hair waved with a side parting, c. 1860.

Longish hair combed in a roll curl in the front, c. 1866.

Short hairstyle with side parting and Dundreary whiskers, c. 1876.

Hair parted at the side with side whiskers, c. 1866.

Short hair with whiskers and small moustache, c. 1862.

Low-crowned hats called 'wide-awakes' had wide brims and were made of felt or straw. Straw hats (with a black band and sometimes known as 'nauticals') were flat crowned with small brims, with ribbon band ends often allowed to hang behind.

Other styles, made of felt, were known as 'deerstalkers', 'pigeon pie' or 'muffin hats', and were worn mainly in the country. From the 1890s straw hats were universally worn. The fashionable 'boater' was made of split straw as well as chip. By about 1898 the brims became narrower. When these hats became popular with the ladies they lost their popularity with the gentlemen who felt them to be effeminate.

For evening wear the 'gibus' top hat remained in vogue throughout the century, and for court wear the cocked hat was still fashionable. This was a crescent shaped hat, meant to be carried flat under the arm. In the 1850s a hard felt hat with a bowl shaped crown, known as a 'bollinger', was originally worn by cabbies, but was adopted by gentlemen for informal wear. The brim could vary in size.

By the 1880s felt bowler hats became taller and for summer wear were of a lighter colour. By the 1890s bowler hats, also sometimes known as 'Derbys', were again less high and the brim turned up all round and curved at the sides. They were generally in either brown or black.

In the 1870s helmet hats or deerstalkers had earflaps and were often made of a checked material and they were worn mainly in the country with Norfolk jackets and knicker-bockers. Other hats worn in the country were of a soft beaver; caps could also be worn. For travelling on trains a fur cap with ear flaps was popular. A Homburg hat was made fashionable about 1889 by the Prince of Wales. It was of stiff felt with the crown indented from the front to the back, similar to a Trilby but made of a softer felt.

Wide-awake hat.

Homburg.

Bollinger hat.

Caps were worn mainly in the country, but from about 1895 they had fuller crowns and a visor in the front and were often worn for golf and tennis as well as school.

ACCESSORIES

Gloves were made of either leather or wool and for evening wear were usually of white or coloured kid leather. By about 1859 coloured gloves were popular amongst fashionable young men. By the 1890s, for town wear, gloves were usually in fawn or grey suede or kid. For evening wear they were usually in a plain white suede with black stitching.

Muffattees or small wrist muffs were sometimes worn in the winter for extra warmth. *Handkerchiefs* when worn for evening wear were embroidered and lace trimmed. They could also be perfumed. In the 1890s they were sometimes of red silk and were only decorative, being worn in the waistcoat.

Canes were usually of ebony or bamboo and were fairly thin with gold or jewelled tops. In the 1850s *umbrellas* were also carried and by the 1880s tightly furled umbrellas began to replace canes. If possible umbrellas were never unrolled as the fashion was for them to be rolled as tightly as possible and used as walking sticks.

A great deal of *jewellery* was worn by men in the evenings, such as elaborate tie pins, shirt studs and gold chains and watches. For day wear ornate tiepins were popular. Ornamental buttons were also fashionable. Eyeglasses (lorgnons) or monocles were also used. The lapel buttonhole often carried flowers. By about 1849 a short watch chain ('Albert') was worn. This was attached to the pocket watch and the other end secured with either a bar or hook to a buttonhole. From about 1888 the Albert watch chain went across from one waistcoat pocket to the other on the opposite side of the front. By the 1890s instead of a watch chain for evening wear, a slim pocket watch was carried in the waistcoat pocket.

Tall bowler hat with petersham band and curled brim, c. 1877.

Bowler hat with the brim curled at the sides, c. 1879.

Victorian Women

*Tall hat decorated with plumes
and feathers with a bow in the
front, c. 1885.*

General Survey

Middle-class ladies wore virtually the same clothes as the upper classes. The characteristic shape of the 1840s was a dress where the bodice pointed towards the low-fitting tightly corseted waist. Shoulders were droopy with tight sleeves; full skirts were almost ground length; bodices were generally joined together and closure was by hooks and eyes at the back. By the 1850s skirts became even wider so that the whole effect resembled a pyramid. The waist was no longer so pinched-in, but the wide skirts had to be supported by a hooped cage. Bodices and skirts were now often separate items.

The invention of the chain-stitch sewing machine and, soon after, the lock-stitch machine by Elais Howe in 1845 (which was the predecessor of the sewing machine) made possible the manufacture of ready-made clothes — a revolution in costume history. With the advent of aniline dyes in about 1860, colours became much brighter.

During the 1860s the main body of the full skirts was pushed back, eventually reviving the bustle. In about 1863 a walking dress was introduced. This had the skirt hitched up to give greater freedom, but at the same time revealed the shoes and stockings, thus encouraging a greater variety of footwear. Bonnets were replaced by hats and by the mid-1860s tight lacing again became fashionable.

In the 1870s dresses became very intricate with skirts draped, arranged and trimmed in rather complicated ways. Skirts became flatter in front and were bunched at the back with, sometimes, a large bow stitched halfway down the back of the skirt. By about 1878 gowns like sheaths had long trains behind elaborately adorned with trimmings, flounces, ribbons, frills, lace, gauging or shirring or any other form of decoration. In all, about 70 metres of trimming could be used on one skirt alone. For evening wear tinsel or other shiny stuffs were also added, making the robes extremely heavy. Until about 1882 the sheath-like dress persisted, causing ladies to hobble about, but in the 1880s large bustles again became popular. They were decorated with all kinds of imitation birds and animals. Bustles reached their maximum size by about 1885-88, not in the gentle curves of previous times, but rather stood out at right angles at the back. About 1889 bustles suddenly lost their popularity.

Tailor-made costumes which had begun to be fashionable from about 1878 gradually developed, especially at first for sport and informal wear as they allowed for more freedom of movement. By the 1890s English tailor-mades were the leaders for morning wear. Plain shirt blouses with variations in sleeves and collars were worn with these tailored costumes.

In the 1890s more decorative bodices were worn with plainer, more practical skirts. This was the result of more sports being played by women. With the advent of cycling the wearing of bloomers was introduced. These were a kind of divided skirt or frilled trouser, originally designed by an American, Mrs Amelia Bloomer, in about 1851.

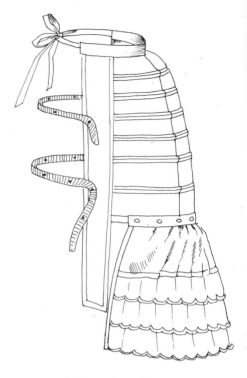

Dimity and steel sprung bustle, c. 1872.

DAY DRESSES

In the 1860s day dresses could be of the separate bodice and skirt variety, or a complete dress without even a waist seam, known as the 'Princess'. The separated style often had the skirt and bodice in different colours. The waist could be raised above the natural waist line in imitation of the Empire style and the neck line could be high ending in a low collar or a V-shaped opening or else a square neck filled in with a chemisette (see Glossary). The latter style could be imitated by a high-necked bodice being decorated with braid forming a square-necked shape — giving a yoke effect. About 1866 it was fashionable to have ribbons and streamers trailing from the neckline at the back. Bodices, which were straight at the waist and met the skirt, were covered by a belt which could be of the same or contrasting material. Sashes tied in a large bow at the back were also very popular in the

The lady is wearing a large three-quarter length travelling coat with bell-shaped sleeves worn over a wide skirted dress. She is also wearing a spoon bonnet tied under the chin with a large bow. The boy wears a belted tunic over knickerbockers. The ankle boots are buttoned on the side. c. 1860.

summer. Swiss belts, which curved to points, above and below, front and back, were generally in black silk or velvet and were either laced or hooked together.

The 'Garibaldi' shirt of the 1860s was the forerunner of a blouse and could be worn tucked into the skirt. A popular colour for the Garibaldi was red with black braiding and buttons. A narrow collar was worn with a silk scarf tucked in and the full sleeves were gathered at the wrist on to a band. This was a style very popular with young ladies from the early 1860s. It could also be worn with a full black skirt with a matching red band around the base and with a braided Zouave jacket or bolero.

Bodices were close fitting with darts each side of the waist. They were long waisted and ended in a point in the front. They could be lined and had three bones issuing fanwise from the waist up and outwards. Fastening was by hooks and eyes at the back, although there could also be buttoning down the front — sometimes open so that the fronts folded back to form revers. Bodices made in a fine material were often not pointed in the front, but were worn with a sash around the waist, the ends of which were allowed to hang loose. Bodices were sometimes padded at the bosom to give a better shape and were often high necked, but could also have a V opening when they were usually filled in with a chemisette or habit shirt. Bodices could be trimmed in a V-shape, from the shoulders down to the point at the waist, in order to emphasise the line. In the 1850s boned bodices became less popular and the points at the waist were replaced by a straighter style by the end of the decade.

The coat bodice of the 1880s was close fitting and could have basques or short tails with hip buttons. Fastening down the front was with buttons, and about 1887 the high neck could be V-shaped and with revers. This style was similar to a man's and was usually worn with a pleated high-necked habit shirt.

By the 1890s it was again lined and boned and had a high collar with fastening either in the front or back. If the bodice had revers, it could be frilled and V-shaped from the shoulder down to the centre waist. Bodices became very wide in the period of enormous sleeves. The yokes were lace and boleros or zouaves were a popular addition, either false or real.

A jacket bodice, the fashion from about 1846, was close fitting, buttoning down the front with short skirts or basques at the waist. The caraco bodice of the 1850s had long basques

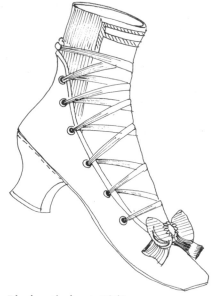

Black satin boot, 1860s.

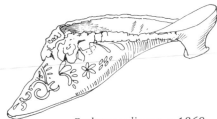

Bedroom slipper, c 1860.

Checked leather shoe with rosette, 1860s.

which extended over the hips, the fronts being slightly curved with rounded corners. The neck opening could be V-shaped or have revers and end with a small collar. Fastening down the front, with ornamental buttons, usually only reached waist level, the rest being left open.

By the 1860s jacket bodices had a waist seam joining the basques to the main body of the bodice. A fitted jacket known as a 'casque' had long basques and wide sleeves. This style was always of the same material as the dress itself. About 1862 a 'corsage postillion', buttoning down the front, and similar to a waistcoat, had short basques at the back only, which gradually became longer, covering the top part of the skirt. This style was later known as a 'Balmoral' bodice.

A style of bodice becoming fashionable from about 1874, called a 'cuirass' bodice, fitted at the normal waistline and was tight, like a corset, and continued over the hips. This style often ended in a point at the front and had a panel of a different colour down the front known as a 'plastron' often matching the tablier of the skirt. The plastron was made to simulate a waistcoat or ruched to suggest a blouse. Tight three-quarter length sleeves were popular with this style of bodice. In about 1881 the cuirass bodice had a 'bag plastron' which was an effect achieved by pouching.

About 1877 a loose blouse was drawn in at the waist with a belt and another style had box pleats front and back and ended just below waist level. In the 1880s the loose blouse could have a yoke at the shoulders with the blouse gathered on to it. Blouses could have small collars and lace frilling down the front.

Around 1877 a Norfolk jacket, similar to the men's in cut, ended at hip level and was usually worn with a trained pleated skirt. This jacket style was again popular in the 1890s when skirts again became plainer.

Another type of jacket, the 'gilet corsage', was made similar to a gentleman's waistcoat. The gilets or waistcoats were fitted and left open and worn with jacket bodices. Sometimes they were made in one with the bodice, being just waistcoat fronts.

Bodice sleeves could be tight fitting and could have an oversleeve or mancherons at the shoulders. Victoria sleeves, with a puff at the elbow, but tight fitting otherwise, were also popular. Bell-shaped sleeves (worn with half under-sleeves), tight to the elbows and then opening out, came into fashion about 1845. The under-sleeves were fastened under the bell sleeves and ended at the wrists with either cuffs or frills known as 'engageantes'.

In the 1850s 'pagoda' sleeves made their appearance. They were fitted at the shoulders and from there immediately expanded out, often being longer at the back. They were later replaced by another style, the 'bishop', which was a full sleeve pleated at the shoulder seam and allowed to hang freely, being gathered on to a band at the wrist. A 'Gabrielle' sleeve consisted of several puffs all the way down from the shoulders to the wrists and ended in closed cuffs.

In the late 1850s most sleeves had epaulettes or 'jockeys' which were decorative ribbon bows at the shoulders. About 1863 a sleeve similar to a man's, with an outer and inner seam, appeared. This type of sleeve was slightly shaped at the elbows, and was tight at the wrists. When it became wider at the shoulders about the mid-1860s it was known as peg topped. In the 1870s the deep cuffs of a coat sleeve could be frilled and they were known as 'mousquetaire' cuffs. From about 1885 the tops of close-fitting sleeves were

Bonnet with crown and brim merging, the sides curving over the ears and the tying strings attached to the inside of the brim, c. 1848.

Both ladies are wearing profusely decorated bonnets tied under the chin. The lady on the left is wearing a carriage cloak over a trained dress. The one on the right is in a day dress with a matching coat. c. 1877-1879.

cut fuller to produce a 'kick-up' effect. These small gigot sleeves expanded to enormous dimensions by about 1895, making the shoulders extremely broad. By 1897 they became much smaller again, retaining some fullness at the top with puffs and flounces, and by the end of the 1890s the shoulder line was smooth and fitted.

In the 1840s the long full skirts just cleared the ground; except for summer wear skirts were always lined. The fullness at the waist was gathered or gauged, more fullness being allowed for the back. The many petticoats beneath gave a dome-shaped appearance. Flounces, which at first were just at the bottom, increased in number and rose higher to the knees. Many skirts had braiding at the hem to protect them against wear. In the summer two skirts could be worn, a shorter one ending at about knee level. Skirts continued to increase in size in the 1850s and were still cut straight, pleated front and sides, and gathered at the back. The base of the skirt became wider, as much as 12-13 metres in circumference. The dome-shaped skirts had to be supported with either hooped petticoats or cage crinolines. They were decorated with multiple flounces, deeper at the top becoming shorter towards the hem, or they could be 'en tablier' (see Glossary). They were also often trimmed in the front with buttons and ribbon bows, which could continue on the bodice.

From about 1860 skirts were gored, straight to cross. The fullness at the waist was more towards the back from about 1865, with the front kept fairly flat. There were inverted pleats in front and box pleats at the back and sides. Most skirts were long and trained. Skirts worn for walking began to be looped up by a variety of devices such as concealed cords, thus revealing the coloured petticoats. From about 1865 double skirts were worn. The outer skirt was hitched up at the sides and to a lesser degree at the back, giving the effect of an apron front. Double skirts, worn mainly for fashionable occasions, lasted until about 1894. There were several styles: an overskirt with a yoke had the underskirt joined to it with box pleats; yet another fashion had a 'peplum', a skirt with a form of drapery sewn to the side seams, which consisted of a length of material narrow at the top and allowed to droop down. An overskirt with an inverted V-opening to reveal the decorated underskirt was also very popular.

In about 1868 pannier skirts had side puffs and were

A walking costume of cloth and velvet edged with fur, c. 1896.

Back view of the popular chiffon blouse and silk skirt outfit, c 1899.

usually worn without a crinoline. These overskirts were sometimes attached to a bodice and known as tunic dresses. Both over and underskirts could be trimmed with ruched ribbons and lace and, from about 1865, scalloped hems, as well as vandyked edges from about 1867, were the mode. Skirts with an overskirt or tunic effect were not made when skirts were tailor-made. Those skirts were usually kilted at the back and sometimes all the way round.

Deep flounces, which had been so popular, were replaced by tiers of narrow frills and braid decorations (the Greek key pattern being the most popular) were also used extensively. From about 1874 skirts were flattened even more in the front with the aid of tapes beneath which were tied back. By the end of the 1870s skirts were no longer full but rather sheath-like with a train until about 1882 when they again expanded behind. The bustle itself was often made of a straw-filled cushion which could be sewn into the back of the skirt and held up by supports. Short flounces arranged in a 'waterfall' fell over the bustle or crinolette, accentuating the back projection. For afternoon wear the trained part of the skirt could be detachable and also raised with loops and string. About 1889, when skirts became less ample, bustles were reduced to pads at the back. For walking, skirts were slightly shorter, sometimes raised 8-10cm from the ground. In the 1890s gored skirts were very popular with the goring enlarged towards the base to give a bell-like flare to about 5 metres, stiffened at the hem with either crin or stiff muslin. This style was without pleats or gathering at the waist.

The 'umbrella' type of skirt was made of a very wide material with only a few gores; it was tight fitting around the hips, this being achieved with darts. The skirt also had quadruple pleats behind and was stiffened around the hem.

An 'Empire' style had straight pieces of material front and back, and inserts of triangular gores at the sides. In the 1890s an accordion pleated skirt, also known as 'sunray' pleating, became very popular. The pleating could be from the waist or have a yoke to knee level and be pleated on to that.

In the 1840s day dresses with bodice and skirt in one came in several styles. The 'pelisse-robe' had trimmings from the shoulders to the point of the bodice at the front and also to the waist at the back. The skirt was either *en tablier* or had a false front. This style of skirt was also part of a close-fitting redingote bodice, fairly plain, with lapels. In the round dress style the bodice was draped across the front, forming a V-shape at the neck, and the skirt was either flounced or *en tablier*. This style was also known just as the robe.

The 'Princess' dress or robe first appeared about 1848 without a waist seam, being cut in one with goring, and became really popular in the 1860s. The back and sides were sometimes pleated to give more fullness; the skirt was usually trained. When double skirts were popular the upper one was always cut in the Princess line, the back being longer than the front to reveal the separate underskirt. In the 1870s the Princess polonaise dress was very popular. The long trained overskirt at the back was draped whilst the sides were looped up, the front being left plain. This style of dress was closed by front buttoning which could be left open from the waist to reveal the underskirt.

About 1870 a style of dress named after Dolly Varden, the heroine in Charles Dickens's *Barnaby Rudge*, was a kind of 'polonaise' dress, the skirt and bodice joined at the waist, the overskirt being short in the front and very bunched out at the sides and back. This style differed in that it was always made in a chintz or cretonne material with the underskirt of brightly coloured cotton or silk in summer, whilst for

Blouse of two-tone silk with velvet bands and rosettes, c. 1896.

Silk blouse with velvet revers and cuffs worn over a chiffon chemisette, c. 1896.

Satin ball dress with bands and bows of velvet. A velvet butterfly bow decorates the skirt front of the dress, c. 1896.

winter wear the heavier flannel or cashmere was printed in chintz-type patterns with the underskirt possibly in a quilted material.

About 1879 a dress made popular by Lily Langtry, the music hall artiste, known as a 'jersey', was made of knitted silk or wool. It was figure hugging to about mid-thigh with a broad belt around the knees. The underskirt was usually untrained and kilted, made of either serge or flannel.

In the 1880s and 1890s most dresses had a separate bodice and skirt except for Princess cuts. A high-waisted style, which was to remain popular until the end of the century, was known as either the 'Directoire' or 'Empire' style. It appeared about 1883 and was made fashionable by the actress Sarah Bernhardt in the play *La Tosca* by Sardou. The high waist effect was accomplished by having a wide sash.

EVENING WEAR

In the 1840s evening dresses had low off-the-shoulder bodices. The décolletage was either straight across or *en coeur* (heart shaped). Horizontal pleats sometimes curved towards the waist and a lace tucker or deep bertha (a wide border made of rows of lace or ribbons which could also cover the shoulders and sleeves) was usual. The bodice was usually pointed and boned. The point at the waist became longer after about 1846 and somewhat resembled that of the 1650s. The short tight sleeves, which had frilled ends, were usually hidden by the deep bertha. The long skirts and knee-length overskirts were similar to those worn in the daytime, but were more elaborately decorated with flounces, ribbons and flowers.

By the 1850s the bodice could also have a V-shaped neckline with a false stomacher, the V-shape being trimmed with several revers or capes. There was always a great amount of decoration used such as artificial flowers, ribbons and lace. The sleeves could also now be *en bouffant*, but they always ended just above the elbows. The 'Princess' style with its low décolletage and ornamentation was worn in the evenings in the 1860s. Evening dresses could also be in separate bodice and skirt styles, bodices being low cut and off-the-shoulders. From about 1865 shoulder straps or ribbon bows were worn instead of sleeves. The skirts, always trained, were usually two in number, the overskirt heavily decorated and looped up to reveal an underskirt which could be trimmed with puffs. From about 1866 peplums (see Glossary) were also popular. Skirt drapery was gradually being replaced by vertical pleats from about 1887, long trains still being in vogue. There were pleated flounces around the bottom of skirts as well as a pleated frill of stiff muslin trimmed with lace on the inside of the skirts, called a 'balayeuse', to keep the skirts out at the back.

For evening dresses in the 1890s the fashion was to follow that of day dresses but with more ornamentation. Broad decorative revers spread over the short puffed sleeves, the kick-up fashion also being popular. About 1895 when the backs of the evening dresses also had a low décolletage, narrow shoulder straps were added, as the large ballooned sleeves were so low on the shoulders that they were unable to support the bodice. Deep lace falls or berthas which fell over the shoulders with shoulder bows or other decorations were very fashionable as well as bolero effects. By 1897 the décolletage was daringly low, the sleeves became less full and were either short and puffed or long and tight fitting to the wrist. About 1895 evening blouses with flared basques and belts became popular. They were similar in style to bodices but less ostentatious. The evening skirts, always trained and about 6 metres around the base were trimmed with cascades of lace. From about 1897 transparent overdresses became very popular.

Dinner dress consisting of a chiffon blouse and a silk skirt, c. 1896

FORMAL WEAR

Wedding dresses were similar in style to day dresses but were made of white silk or satin with lace trimmings, Brussels being a favourite. A veil and orange blossom wreaths were also fashionable. Bridesmaids usually wore pastel colours. In the 1860s the bodice could be high necked or, if the décolletage were low, filled in with a chemisette. The head veil usually covered the face. By the 1880s the bodice was usually high to the neck and the sleeves long, the skirt also being long and trained. The material could be, apart from satins and silk, of velvet. The veil became very long, sometimes almost reaching the ground.

For *mourning* black bombazine with crêpe and jet trimmings was considered most appropriate. In the 1870s black crêpe decorated everything — bodices, skirts and coats. Black crêpe veils were worn over bonnets. Gloves as well as handkerchiefs were also in black. When in half mourning a little white material was permissible.

Tea gown in crépon with a deep lawn collar bordered with lace, c. 1896.

The lady is wearing a sailor type dress with a sailor collar which is made in the Princess line.

The 'peignoir' which was a form of negligee or morning dress was similar to the pelisse robe with bishop-style sleeves; the open front, with revers, revealed the underdress. This was not worn as a dressing gown but rather for informal occasions. In the 1870s the 'tea gown', cut in the Princess style, was fairly loose, so that tight-fitting corsets were not necessary. Tea gowns were worn when ladies changed from their more formal day dresses in the afternoon to relax before donning their evening finery. Tea gowns were even worn when afternoon tea became a social function and gentlemen were present. They were sometimes made with a watteau sac back and trained, with the sleeves ending at the elbows in ruffles.

In the 1880s tea gowns became extremely elaborate and by about 1888 they were also made in the Empire style with a rounded yoke and sash, the sleeves quite long with hanging ends almost reaching the ground. By the 1890s the fronts could be trimmed with masses of lace, forming a jabot (see Glossary). By the end of the century the short-waisted Empire tea gown often had a transparent overdress pleated on to a short yoke.

A *riding* costume consisted of a skirt and bodice separate. The jacket was closed at the neck with a small turned-over collar and lapels, and if worn open revealed a habit shirt which buttoned down the front. The skirt was long and trained.

For *shooting* Norfolk jackets with knee-length skirts were worn under which were knickerbockers and garters.

In the 1860s dark-blue serge was popular for *yachting*. A coloured handkerchief could be worn around the neck. At about the same time a *bathing* costume consisted of body and trousers cut in one and made of a stout material, the style similar to combinations with a short overskirt often added. The high necks could be adorned with sailor collars. In the 1880s bathing costumes consisted of a long tunic over drawers which were gathered at the ankles. The tunic could have short sleeves. By about 1866 the costumes could be made of stockingette with a detachable skirt. In the 1890s the trousers became shorter and a tunic with a belt was worn over the one-piece trouser and bodice ensemble.

For *tennis*, walking dresses were worn until about 1888, when blouse and skirt reaching the ankles became the fashion.

The short jacket worn over a frilled blouse and bloomers is worn for bicycling, c. 1894.

3 The distinction between classes showed very strongly in the dress of children. *Left*, a boy dressed in the Eton suit complete with mortar board and hat. *Centre left*, a 'firewood' girl dressed in the hand-me-downs of an adult. *Centre*, the figure of the popular hurdy-gurdy man with his portable puppet show. *Centre right*, a little flower girl, again wearing the cast-offs of an elder sister. *Right*, a boy of the middle class dressed in the favourite fashion of sailor suit.

4 *Left*, a young lady with high necked and waisted bustle dress over which is a light mantle following the contours of the dress. *Centre*, a fashionable man-about-town in summer gear – high buttoned jacket with short lapels, butterfly shirt collar with cravat and straw 'boater' hat. *Right*, a bustle dress with short, waisted velvet jacket edged with fur and close-fitting hat in matching material.

Black canvas shoes and a jockey cap as well as gloves completed the outfit. In the 1880s *cycling* outfits consisted of short jacket bodices or Norfolk jackets and box pleated skirts which could be weighted with lead. Later, in the 1890s, a short jacket or waistcoat was worn with a blouse beneath and instead of a skirt which could blow up in the wind, knickerbockers or bloomers were more practical. A jockey cap or bowler hat was also worn.

OUTDOOR WEAR

Shawls were worn and made in a variety of sizes, often with fringed borders. For summer wear they were of lighter materials such as silks or embroidered organdy, and in winter of woollen materials such as cashmere. Paisley designs were particularly popular.

Capes hung from the shoulders to the waist or thigh whilst mantles were fitted to the shoulders and had concealed slits for the arms. They also often had Medici collars and could be yoked and long, reaching to the ground. There were a variety of loose or semi-fitting capes and mantles with innumerable names. Basically they all hung loosely from the neck to the knees with either loose sleeves or slits for the arms. Some of the named sorts of the 1840s were: the 'paletot', a three-caped mantle with arm slits, and the 'pelerine-mantle' with broad front panels edged with frills. For evening the 'burnoise' had short sleeves and a hood. A 'feather pelerine' was made of feathers stitched on to a canvas backing. Shawl-mantles fitted around the neck and shoulders and were allowed to hang loosely down to the hem over the wide skirts of the 1850s. A 'talma-mantle' or cloak had either a hood or collar with tassels.

In the 1860s cloaks were usually three-quarter length with slight shaping to the waist, then falling over the wide skirts; they could also have pagoda-like sleeves. There were also circular cloaks in various lengths, without sleeves but sometimes with a cape and, from about 1878, a hood. A 'Balmoral mantle' was similar to an Inverness cape, the cape being incomplete at the back, the fronts sewn into the side seams of the loose coat. Balmorals were so called to commemorate Queen Victoria's association with Balmoral Castle, Scotland.

In the 1880s long mantles were usually shaped to the waist at the back with tapes inside. Medici collars were also worn. The mantles had a kick-up effect at the shoulders

Flannel bathing costume consisting of a short sleeved tunic and sash worn over drawers that were gathered just above the ankles, c. 1881.

from about 1889. In the 1890s when dress sleeves were excessive, mantles, cloaks and capes were the chief outdoor attire. They could be of almost any length, plain or tiered, and cut gored or circular and fitted at the shoulders with darts. From about 1895 mantles could be caped with bishop sleeves; large collars which could be wired to stand away were also very popular.

'Pardessus' or paletot were names given to any outdoor garment that had sleeves, the paletot being more shaped. In the 1840s the 'sortie-de-bal' (also applied to evening cloaks in the 1850s) was an unshaped evening coat, bell sleeved and often fur trimmed. From about 1850 many coats, jackets, Ulsters and Invernesses as well as riding habits were made by tailors and were mainly based on men's styles. The 'pelisse' was a three-quarter length waisted overcoat worn from the 1850s with bell-shaped sleeves. The 'pelisse-mantle' was double-breasted, not shaped and had a wide collar and short sleeves ending in cuffs. The paletot of the 1860s could be single or double-breasted, shaped to the waist or straight, with coat sleeves, three-quarter length or short. When short it was sometimes called a yachting jacket, the name paletot being reserved for the longer variety. Short loose 'zouave' jackets with square fronts and military braid decoration, were also very popular. They were often decorated with braids in the military manner. Short sealskin and beaver jackets first appeared in the 1870s. Until about 1875 jackets were usually close fitting just at the back, after which they were fitted all round. If they became knee length they could be single or double-breasted with turned-down collars and short lapels. If, however, jackets were short the sleeves were often in the 'pagoda' style (see Glossary) as well as in the coat sleeve mode, which was more usual for longer jackets. The loose type of double-breasted jacket was known as a 'reefer' and also had coat sleeves. Jackets could also have vents at the back and came in the same material as the dresses with which they were worn, thus completing the outfits.

In the 1890s jackets could be close fitting or sac-backed with wide revers and wide sleeves which sometimes had to be drawn down with sleeve-tongs. From about 1876 a paletot made in the style of a Princess robe ended just above the skirt hem. They were slightly trained, usually being worn over trained dresses. They had turned-down collars and lapels and could be fur trimmed. Single or double-breasted,

Undersleeve made of muslin and ribbon, 1860s.

Detatchable lace undersleeve for a chemisette, 1850s.

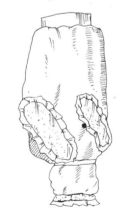

Detatchable sleeve for a chemisette, 1850s.

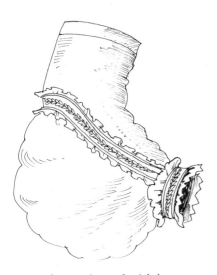

Dress sleeve trimmed with lace, 1860s.

they were closed with buttons from the neck to hem, but sometimes left open from the waist down. The sleeves were of the coat variety, being made with two seams. Patch pockets were quite usual.

Other coats known as 'Ulsters' or waterproofs were waisted and could have a half-belt behind and also sometimes a back vent. The coat sleeves were close fitting. They could have either a hood or capes attached. 'Chesterfield' coats appeared about 1878 and were ground length and fitted. They were usually single-breasted with turned-down collars and lapels which could be faced with velvet. (In the early 1890s Chesterfields were in the masculine style.) In the 1880s the waisted styles of overcoats were made to fit over bustles. One of the styles, the 'Dolman', close fitting at the back, was allowed to hang straight in the front, being fastened at the neck. They had shawl-like sleeves and when they were short were known as 'mantlets' and when long were called 'Dolman-pelisses'. They were lavishly trimmed with lace, ruching and jet. In the 1880s fur coats became fashionable.

Three-quarter length coats were fashionable throughout the 1890s and could be single or double-breasted and be loose with sac backs or fitted. During the period of large sleeves on dresses, the coat sleeves were also widened. Covert coats with loose backs were popular with the tailor-made costumes.

DRESS ACCESSORIES

Chemisettes or bodice fill-ins sometimes had sleeves which could take the place of engageantes or half-sleeves, and were worn under bell or pagoda sleeves. When in the same material as the dress they were also known as double sleeves. For morning wear sleeves usually ended in cuffs, but on other occasions they were often open or lace frilled.

Separate turned-down lace-edged collars were worn with high-necked bodices and closed with a brooch, ribbon bow or cravat. Silk scarves became fashionable about 1861. Jabots (see Glossary), from the 1880s, also decorated the fronts of bodices and blouses. Fichus, which were trimmed with lace, were worn with V-necked openings. The ends were often crossed in the front and then pinned or tied behind. Berthas and small Elizabethan-style ruffs were also fashionable in the 1870s. Habit shirts, similar to chemisettes, were very popular with day dresses.

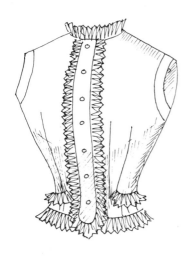

Chemisette, c. 1852.

UNDERWEAR

In the 1840s tight-laced corsets were an important feature as were crinolines in achieving the dome shape and several petticoats were also worn, both flannel and cotton. In the 1850s corsets became shorter and not quite so tightly laced, apart from when worn under evening attire, but under the sheath dresses of the late 1870s long tight-laced corsets again became popular. From the 1840s to 1860s the crinoline or bustle dominated dress; as the sleeves decreased in size so the skirts expanded. Horsehair or crin petticoats were worn until the late 1840s when these were replaced by whalebone, steel or cane hoops suspended by vertical tapes.

Bustles made of crin were worn until the crinoline was developed. Crinolines were first dome shaped in the 1850s becoming more pyramidical in the 1860s. When the style became too cumbersome the crinoline became flatter in the front with the fullness being pushed towards the back. When it reached its limit the crinoline subsided with the material just being draped and to support this a bustle or tournure made of horsehair was worn over a small crinoline. This was discarded in the early 1870s, being replaced by an elongated bustle or crinoline.

By about 1875 the bustle was also unfashionable, as the mode was now for slim hips and sheath dresses. The drapery of the dress was all that remained, together with a trained petticoat. In the early 1880s the bustle returned as drapery around the hips and a wider skirt again became popular. A crinolette or half crinoline was worn which made the skirt at the back stand out almost at right angles. Skirts for this type of undergarment were gored with the fullness at the waist gathered or pleated at the back.

Trousers had to be worn beneath crinolines as they were so stiff that when moving they could sway so high that the legs were revealed, and when climbing stairs crinolines could even reveal the legs to knee height — a shocking prospect for Victorian ladies, if not men. Mrs Amelia Bloomer in 1851 designed a type of frilled trouser, known as bloomers, which, after initial resistance, became almost legendary.

FOOTWEAR

In the 1840s low heels were popular for shoes whilst the heels of boots were slightly higher. For formal occasions,

Close fitting corset, c. 1870.

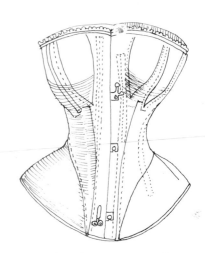

Victoria corset, c. 1863.

Knee length drawers, 1860s.

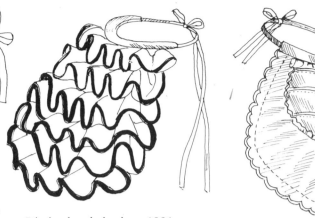

Dimity bustle back, c. 1881.

Crinoline bustle, c. 1872.

Haircloth bustle, c. 1881.

silk, satin or kid slippers were worn. Boots for evening wear became fashionable about 1847 and were mainly of white satin with black toecaps. Boots with cashmere tops and leather vamps were worn for walking. Bedroom slippers began to make their appearance. Small rosettes or jewelled buckles and buttons were added as ornamentation.

By the 1850s shoes and boots were low heeled, although evening shoes did have higher heels. Evening slippers, ballet-pump shaped, had low or flat heels. They were usually made of a material and had thin soles.

Boots were normally worn out of doors and were fairly short, usually made of material with patent-leather trimmings. They were often laced on the inner side or buttoned with button hooks on the outer. If neither type of fastening was used they were elastic sided, a style reserved for informal wear. Among many styles of boots in the 1850s were 'Balmorals', which were thick soled with a military-type heel and laced-up front, either side of which could be decorated with perforations. These were always worn with dresses hitched up over petticoats. 'Adelaides' were boots with fringed tops, while 'Polish' boots were high and tasselled with heels of a different colour. Pattens were still worn, but mainly in the country, whilst galoshes and overshoes were worn in rainy weather.

As day dresses became shorter in the 1860s, shoes and boots played a more important role in fashion, as they were now more visible. Toes became more squared or rounded with heels 2-3cm high. Shoes were in a variety of colours or else matched the dresses. The upper parts of shoes became longer with a ribbon bow or rosette on the toes. Trimmings of all kinds such as Moorish crescents or jewellery were also very popular. Cork soles with wool linings were often worn inside boots. 'Cromwell' shoes (favoured for croquet parties where shorter skirts enabled pretty shoes and ankles to be admired) had large square brass or silver buckles over an instep with a high tongue. Boots reaching above the ankles, made of various types of leather and material with tasselled tops and decorated insteps, were very fashionable.

In the 1870s calf-length high-heeled boots which laced up the front were usually worn in black, with astrakhan fur a popular trimming in winter. Shoes became more popular than boots and could be slipper shaped with long uppers and lacing over a tongue. Fashionable shoes were matched to the stockings and dresses. For evening wear they were often of a soft white leather worn with white stockings, which could be clocked. The shoes themselves could also be embroidered in coloured silks, gold or silver. Boots were seldom worn in the evenings, becoming less popular even for day wear by about 1883.

With the advent of the Dolly Varden hats, *c.* 1871, floral patterned materials became popular. Shoes followed the fashionable trend and were fastened with a bar and button fastening. By the 1880s rounded toes and lower heels were again fashionable with front lacing and patent-leather toecaps and were usually in black or bronze. A type of shoe known as 'Magpie' because of its colouring, was of black patent leather with white buckskin, the heels low and square. This was popular from about 1885. For evening wear Louis heels again became popular.

For day wear 'Oxfords', laced up the front, were practical and popular. Cromwell shoes became fashionable for walking about 1889 with their high fronts fastened with buckles and decorated with large bows.

In the 1850s cotton, lisle or silk openwork *stockings* were worn, but as these were hidden beneath the skirts, they did not become an important feature until later when dresses became shorter. By the 1860s a new type of stocking was introduced which had the seam and stocking knitted in one. With shoes the stockings worn were usually plain white, whereas with boots they could be coloured, spotted or patterned. Plaid stockings were also very popular for 'walking-out'.

Towards the end of the 1880s cotton and ribbed cashmere as well as plain lisle stockings with coloured clocks were

Young girl's high boot, 1860s.

Lady's bootee, c. 1860.

Mule, c. 1860.

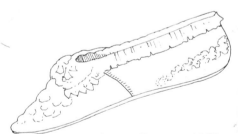

Bedroom slipper, c. 1860.

Lady's bootee, c. 1860.

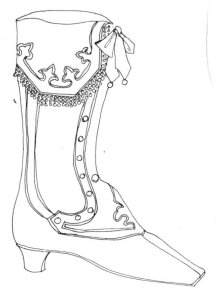

worn, although for afternoon wear it was more stylish to have silk stockings with designs embroidered on the front. For evening wear, black silk was the fashionable mode from about 1888, before which white silk openwork was popular, as were ribbed stockings.

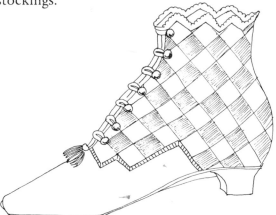

Embroidered Russian style high boot, 1860s.

Checked leather boot, the top edged with lace, 1860s

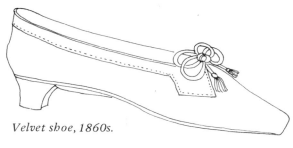

Velvet shoe, 1860s.

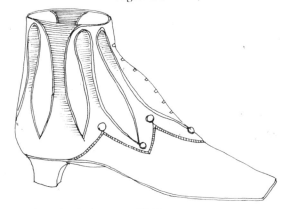

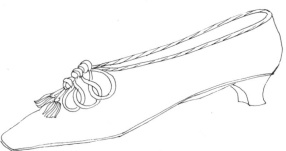

Boot with a cuff, c 1860.

Leather elastic boot, c. 1860.

Patent leather shoe, 1860s.

Shoe of kid leather with front cross lacing, c. 1875.

55

Small *caps* could be worn indoors in the daytime but were not so popular as they had been previously and ceased to be worn by the younger generation by the 1880s. They were worn on the back of the head and were trimmed with lace or frills, more so at the sides, sometimes forming lappets. By the 1850s caps were often of the 'fanchon' type (half kerchiefs) and were decorated with ribbons hanging behind, sometimes with lappets. By about 1855 young ladies discarded even these and often only wore ribbons in their hair.

In the 1860s *hair nets* (often decorated with beads) were worn to contain the chignon (see Glossary). In the 1840s caps for evening wear were lavishly decorated with flowers and lace as well as jewels. Lace fanchons were also draped over the head.

Turbans, which had previously been so popular, became much smaller in the 1840s and had the ends hanging over the shoulders, but by far the most popular fashion was hair decoration, silk nets and combs also being popular. *Toques*, turban-like hats, again became fashionable in the 1880s and were in varying shapes from inverted flower pots to gable shapes, sometimes trimmed with fur or feathers.

In the 1850s Spanish hats were made fashionable by the Empress Eugénie and were of velvet with a feather at the side. Velvet *hair bands*, *coronets* and *diadems* were also very popular as well as jewelled *pins* and butterflies in the 1870s. In the 1880s small caps were worn as a basis for the elaborate decorations of feathers, flowers, fruit and jewels.

Bonnets in the 1840s were the most popular of headwear for outdoors, though compared with the 1830s there were fewer decorations. *Bavolets* (see Glossary) were always worn, although mentonnières (see Glossary) were superseded by flowers and other frilling sewn on the inside of the brims, sometimes right round to encompass the face. Brims often merged with the crown and the bonnet strings, which were attached to the brim, brought the brim down to frame the face. About 1848 an extra removeable brim known as an 'ugly' was sometimes added. It was made of silk stretched over half hoops of cane and could be folded back like a calash. Veils were sometimes added to the back of bonnets and could be left to hang behind or draped over the face.

By about 1853 bonnets had become smaller and were worn further back on the head, sometimes being held in place with a velvet bandeau. A 'Mary Stuart' style bonnet with

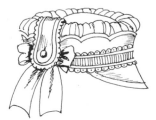

Military type cap with a peak and loop and button decoration, c. 1854.

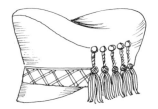

Military type cap with a peak and tassels, c. 1854.

Muslin night cap, c. 1872.

Jockey hat with tassels.

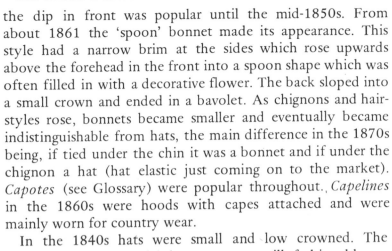

top left: serrated straw bonnet
with bavolet. c. 1870s.

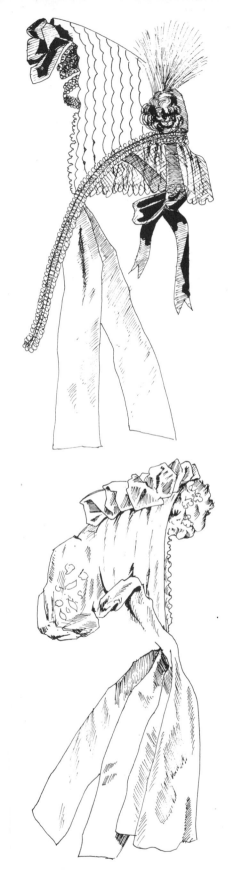

the dip in front was popular until the mid-1850s. From about 1861 the 'spoon' bonnet made its appearance. This style had a narrow brim at the sides which rose upwards above the forehead in the front into a spoon shape which was often filled in with a decorative flower. The back sloped into a small crown and ended in a bavolet. As chignons and hairstyles rose, bonnets became smaller and eventually became indistinguishable from hats, the main difference in the 1870s being, if tied under the chin it was a bonnet and if under the chignon a hat (hat elastic just coming on to the market). *Capotes* (see Glossary) were popular throughout. *Capelines* in the 1860s were hoods with capes attached and were mainly worn for country wear.

In the 1840s hats were small and low crowned. The 'gypsy' hat or 'Pamela' bonnet were still fashionable, as were straw or chip hats. About 1854 a large hat known as a 'round hat' became popular, its low mushroom-shaped crown and large brim trimmed with ribbons which were permitted to hang loosely behind. The ribbons attached to the crown beneath the brim were often held in the hands to prevent the hat from blowing off in the wind. The 'mousquetaire', also mushroom shaped, was usually made of stiff brown straw with a lace edging around the brim and was popular at the same time.

Top hats with deep crowns, either flat or round topped, and with brims, were mainly worn for riding and were often decorated with ribbon and buckles or feathers. 'Bergère' straw hats, low crowned and soft brimmed, low crowned sailor hats with stiff brims and hats with flower pot crowns were all fashionable in the 1860s. After about 1865 most hats were small and flat.

'Glengarry' caps and pork pie hats became popular at the same time, as the chignon became higher at the back, so these styles were worn tilted forward. Fashionable modes were the Dolly Varden small crowned leghorn hats with a limp brim decorated with ribbon trimmings and streamers hanging down the back. A small sailor-type hat with a turned-up brim was also popular. Until about 1875 short veils on headwear were fashionable, but after then they became longer and could be draped around the head and neck, the ends crossed behind and tied in a bow at the front.

Around 1883 gable hats or bonnets with the brim pointing up sharply were fashionable, and about 1887 the crown also became high in a flower-pot style. Then, from about 1889,

bottom left: bonnet trimmed with ribbons.

crowns could be flatter with stiff flat brims or 'mushroom style'. Trimmings in the 1880s were excessive, with the use of ribbons, flowers, foliage, birds and insects. From about 1895 brims of a contrasting colour to the crowns could be of a stiffened and pleated material and after about 1897 hats again became larger with the brims sometimes turned up in the front to give a halo effect.

Windsor hat with a short veil.

Small lace trimmed cap with side lappets, c. 1868.

Bonnet with a bavolet and lacing around the inside of the brim, c. 1862.

Small day cap with streamers. The hair is parted in the centre and sleekly combed with plaits looped up at the sides, c. 1860.

HAIRSTYLES

In the early 1840s sleeker hair was popular. Macassar oil was used so that hair would lie flat either side of a centre parting, the hair then being pulled back into a chignon or bun which was kept in place with a large ivory or tortoise-shell comb or hairpins. For evening wear the hair could be ornamented with flowers, lace, feathers or jewellery. Young girls, however, did not use so much hair decoration.

Ringlets were also very fashionable, not only at the sides, but also sometimes at the back. Hair was profusely decorated with ribbons and bows as well as flowers; even jewellery was entwined in the chignon or back hair which could also be covered with a gold or silver chenille net. To add width, puffs of fine material were also worn at the sides. In the 1840s day and evening styles were similar, with the exception that

Hat worn tilted forward and decorated with feathers, c. 1898.

Type of top hat trimmed with ribbons and feathers, c. 1887.

Lace hat with hourglass crown, and upright trimming of lace in the front, c. 1896.

for evening wear long curls were more popular.

Popular styles had front hair combed sleekly down either side from a centre parting and then either plaited and placed around each ear in a circlet, or draped around the ears forming a bun at the back of the head. Side hair could also be in ringlets with more false ones added for evening wear. The back hair, however, was always twisted and worn in a knot or chignon at the back. Hair could be kept up with combs and hairpins. After about 1840 'feronnières' (see Glossary) which had been fashionable were no longer worn.

In the 1850s hair was worn parted in the centre with the sides slightly puffed out and a chignon or bun at the nape of the neck. To give height the hair could be placed over pads (Mary Stuart style). Side hair could be waved with the use of heated iron tongs, only young girls wearing side ringlets. For evening wear the hair was highly decorated and sometimes a plait of artificial hair was placed around the head like a coronet. In the late 1850s hairstyles became plainer with a fuller chignon at the nape of the neck held in place with a net. This remained the mode until the 1860s. The chignon was the most important feature of this decade, consisting mainly of massed curls or plaits or vertical curls fastened down. Much artificial hair was used to supplement natural hair. The chignon gradually became higher on the head with one or two ringlets allowed to fall down. The centre parting was still worn with the side hair puffed out, plaited or looped around the ears, with the ends added to the bun at the back. Hair could, on occasion, be brushed straight back rather than parted in the centre.

In the early part of the 1860s gold-coloured hair powder was popular, worn to resemble the colour of the French Empress Eugénie's hair. In the late 1860s hairstyles were fairly flat on top with the sides waved and the back hair coiled and held up with a slide. Another fashion, from France, had the hair at the back hanging loose in ringlets.

In the 1870s hair was brushed away from the sides, and a slight fringe could be worn with the back hair worn high, falling in locks. Side hair was added to a chignon if one was worn, but the ears were left uncovered. For evening wear the hair was worn up with a topknot of flowers and ribbons. False hair was used to accomplish the complicated styles.

In the 1880s the bun or chignon was no longer worn at the nape, but higher on the head, and a fringe, which was curly, as well as ringlets over the ears were very popular.

59

When a bonnet was worn over this hairstyle, it was reminiscent of the 'fontange' of the seventeenth and eighteenth centuries. If the hair was naturally straight, false hair curls were added. A new method, known as 'Marcel' waving and invented by a Parisian hairdresser named Marcel Grateau, consisted of the use of special heated pointed tongs which allowed the waves to remain at least a few days. This was the forerunner of permanent waving which came into vogue about 1904 and was invented by a German in England named Karl Ludwig Nessler, the son of a German shoemaker.

Lily Langtry, who had a great influence on fashion, wore her hair waved with a low chignon at the back, and as her hair was blonde, this colour also became very popular, and, until the end of the century, hair was often dyed in that colour. Made up hairpieces called 'frizzettes' and 'scalpettes' were in great demand, whilst small curls were glued to the forehead. By the mid-1880s false hair was unfashionable.

The 'catagan' style worn in the 1870s (a lopped plait at the nape of the neck) was held in place with a ribbon bow, and was now worn mainly by younger people and schoolgirls in the 1880s. From about 1896 a style with projecting loops high at the back of the head was very fashionable. The back hair could also be combed up, the ears always being left uncovered.

Hairstyle with a chignon at the back and decorated with a ribbon, c. 1868.

MAKE-UP

In the 1840s rouge was applied sparsely, a pearl powder being used to give pallor to the skin. Lavender water or eau de Cologne was used in preference to heavy perfumes in the 1850s. In the 1860s it became fashionable to use golden coloured hair powder in order to imitate the colour of Empress Eugénie's hair.

ACCESSORIES

Aprons were worn informally at home and were usually of a satin or similar material, embroidered or lace edged. Small aprons known as 'fig leaves' came into fashion in the 1860s and continued into the 1880s from which time embroidered aprons with bibs could be worn for breakfast and with tea gowns. After the late 1880s they were not fashionable any more except for servants who wore them only for domestic duties. Metal clips in fancy shapes, known as 'pages', were attached to a chain worn around the waist and were used to hold up skirts when walking. *Handkerchiefs* for evening wear were usually lace edged with rounded corners. For day

Hair worn piled high, but tied low at the nape of the neck in a 'catagan' style, c. 1877.

Front view of above c. 1877.

Back hair worn high with a small fringe in the front, c. 1877.

Topknot of flowers with the hair brushed away from the ears and allowed to hang in ringlets, c. 1876.

wear decorative handkerchiefs could have coloured borders or embroidered corners. *Gloves* for day wear were quite short and plain in the 1840s whilst evening gloves were trimmed at the wrists with lace or ruching. In the 1850s they became tight fitting as small hands were considered 'well bred'; this necessitated buttoning at the wrists. For country wear gloves could have gauntlets, whilst for town wear they might be trimmed with ribbons at the wrists and the stripes at the back could be of contrasting colour. Fur *boas* became fashionable about 1869. They could also be made to match muffs and were sometimes of feathers, some being about 3 metres long. Folding *fans*, sometimes made of sandal wood were popular, often with painted scenes. They had very decorative handles, sometimes of mother-of-pearl. From the 1870s fans became much larger and could be made of ostrich feathers. The handles could also be made of tortoiseshell or ivory.

Parasols were fairly small, embroidered and fringed. They could be pagoda shaped with long and delicate or short and thick handles. In the 1880s they became dome shaped and could be lined and lace edged, often in a material matching the dresses. From about 1888 handles could have crystal or china knobs.

Jewellery was not so popular in the 1840s. Popular, however, were cut steel or other metal 'chatelaines' (see Glossary) which were functional. They were basically chains from which were suspended decorative shields with several shorter chains from which hung utilitarian items, some in sheaths, such as needles, scissors, watches, seals and smelling salts. Gold watches, some with enamelled backs could be suspended from a chain around the neck. Bracelets were fashionable and could contain a miniature portrait or lock of hair in a container. In the 1860s dog-collar type necklaces of wide bands of velvet with coloured beads or semi-precious gems became very fashionable. Long pendant earrings were also popular, as well as cameo necklaces, bracelets and rings. Jet, a common stone, was much used in all kinds of decoration. About 1865 'benoiton' chains, popularised by the play 'La Famille Benoiton' by Sardou, were filigree chains of gold, silver or jet hanging from the hair or chignon down either side over the shoulders on to the bosom. Decorated buttons in cut steel or jet were also very fashionable. Coronets and tiaras were popular for evening wear as were pearls worn in necklaces and drop earrings. These were made fashionable by the Empress Eugénie whose favourite jewel was the pearl. Lockets or crosses could be worn on a velvet ribbon around the neck when the décolletage was low. Gold and silver necklaces were also fashionable and garnets and opals were amongst the most popular semi-precious stones used.

Velvet chatelaine pocket suspended from a chain.

Small bag with a bow decoration suspended from the waist. c. 1876.

Handbag which could be carried over the arm, c. 1879.

Victorian Children

The small boy is in a reefer jacket with Fauntleroy type collar and cuffs, and a skirt. The high boots are buttoned on the outside, c. 1893.

Boys

A *tunic suit* worn by small boys from the 1840s was a close-fitting jacket with the skirts either pleated or gathered at the waist, reaching to the knees. It was closed in the front with buttons and could have a belt. Boys up to the age of about six wore drawers with frilled ends showing beneath, and were dressed like little girls, with their hair also quite long. Boys a little older usually wore trousers. In the 1850s gingham blouses were popular and were worn with trousers that could have a silk stripe on the outside seams. Knitted stockings were also fashionable as well as boots with elastic sides.

Knickerbocker suits were very popular from the 1860s. The jacket was short without a collar, and on older boys a waistcoat could be worn underneath. Knickerbockers were baggy breeches which were fastened at the knees with a band and buckle.

Sailor suits, also fashionable in the same period, consisted of knickerbockers with a blouse that had a large square collar around a V-necked opening filled in with a vest worn beneath. A nautical straw hat usually finished off the outfit. Knitted jersey suits were worn from the 1860s onwards often with knitted stocking caps, known as 'brewers' caps or 'fisherman's' caps.

Reefer jackets which were double-breasted with lapels and worn with knickerbockers were favoured by young boys from the 1870s, whilst from the 1880s, blazers, usually made of flannel, were worn unlined and in plain colours or a striped design. If the blazers were in a plain material the edges could be bound with coloured ribbon or braid, different schools having their own colours. The jacket had three patch pockets and the collar was of the stepped variety. The three buttons could either be of gilt or covered in the blazer material. They were worn mainly for school or sports such as cricket or tennis.

At the same period Norfolk jackets and knitted fishermen's caps were worn by boys as well as navy blue jerseys which had previously only been worn by fishermen. Knee breeches became tight fitting, being buttoned just beneath the knees. Tweed was a popular material used from 1885.

After Mrs Hodgson Burnett wrote *Little Lord Fauntleroy* in 1886, velvet party suits named after the hero became very fashionable. The top was a short type of tunic with short skirts encircled with a wide sash, the ends hanging to one side. Around the neck was a white lace collar, so large that it hung to the shoulders. This was matched by lace cuffs at the wrists resembling Cavalier period fashion. Knickerbockers were worn as were plumed hats and long hair completed the ensemble.

For boys, a new type of trouser — 'shorts' — came into fashion in about 1895. Made in all kinds of material, they were, by 1900, worn with matching jackets, thus forming short trousered suits.

Girls

Pelisses were very fashionable as well as cottage style bonnets ornamented with ribbons and feathers.

Hair was usually parted in the centre with the sides tied up in ribbons and sometimes an artificial flower was also worn as decoration. This hairstyle was popularised by Queen Victoria and remained in fashion for over 20 years.

Dresses were similar to those of grown-ups and coats closed down to the waist and were then allowed to fall open to prevent the full skirt of the dress beneath from being crushed. Short capes were also fashionable. Although dress skirt lengths varied, longer ones were more general at the start of this period. Bodices had large collars and aprons were still popular as an accessory throughout the period.

In the 1850s older girls had their hair with a centre parting and done in a chignon at the nape of the neck, covered with a net, or else the side hair could be plaited or coiled around the ears with sometimes artificial flowers for ornamentation.

Young girl wearing a high necked and smocked and embroidered summer dress with dark stockings and shoes with patent leather toecaps and heels, c. 1896.

The little girl is wearing an overcoat with gigot sleeves and a hat with a lace frill and bow decoration on top, c. 1896.

Poke bonnets were going out of fashion and were replaced with large brimmed, but small crowned leghorn (straw) hats with a ribbon around the crown, the ends left dangling at the back. They were held on with a ribbon tied under the chin.

Dresses became high necked except for party wear, skirts having several layers of frills. Long sleeves became bell shaped and often had wrist frills. Coats and jackets were fashionable with fur trimmings.

Elastic-sided boots were worn on many occasions and when worn for parties could have patent-leather heels and toecaps. White stockings were usual until the 1850s, whilst younger children could wear striped ones. From about 1870 dark woollen stockings were worn as well.

No child went out of doors without some head covering which was usually similar to that worn by adults. Little girls did wear sailor hats in the 1860s like boys.

Towards the 1860s crinolines became larger with skirts bunched up. Pantaloons became less popular in the 1860s and loose drawers usually of white cambric which peeped beneath the frocks were worn instead. Drawers were worn mainly as underwear but were lace edged.

Hair in the late 1860s was worn brushed away from the forehead and allowed to hang loosely down with a ribbon around the head. Fringes gradually became popular and were worn more and more. Hats became much smaller with these hairstyles.

In the very early 1870s both panniers and crinolines, having reached their greatest dimensions, suddenly became quite unfashionable, as also did the large sleeves which were replaced by tight-fitting ones. These could be puffed all the way down as the earlier fashion 'en bouffant'. Puffed shoulder sleeves were very popular for girls' party dresses.

Fichus were very popular in the 1870s, as were shoulder capes worn over coats; muffs were a fashionable accessory.

Between about 1875 and 1880 the backs of skirts became an important feature of dress. They were puffed out by means of layer upon layer of frills and bows. Overskirts could be of a contrasting colour, gathered at the back, but tight across the front. Apron effects were very fashionable. A draped overskirt style known as the 'fishwife' style was with the bodice in one and the underskirt in a different colour. The overskirt could also be gathered up slightly in the front. To make the back extend even more, padding could be used, as well as sashes, knots and extra pieces of material.

Pleats and frills were very popular as decoration as well as braids which had been in use for some time. The neck of the bodice was usually high and close fitting with a frill being more usual than a collar.

Hats again became larger with goffered frills, flowers and ribbon trimmings. Small straw hats often had large bows in the front and tam-o-shanters were also still being worn by girls as well as boys.

Smocking on frocks was very popular from the 1880s until the end of the century. This was a type of embroidery whereby stitches divide and hold together alternately tiny pleats to give a honeycomb effect.

By the 1890s the bustle effect at the back was less popular, although decorative aprons were still being worn.

Kate Greenaway's illustrations in the 1890s revived for a brief period the Empire look with high waisted dresses and long coats with cape collars. Buttoned boots were popular whilst striped stockings were worn less towards the end of the century.

Child's corset, 1860s.

Glossary

Bag Plastron	Sometimes worn in place of a waistcoat front, the front panel of a bodice, sagging in front.
Balayeuse	Stiff frilling to protect the inside hem of a skirt.
Bavolet	Curtain at the back of bonnet.
Bell sleeve	Close fitting to the elbow, then expanding into a bell shape.
Bertha	Silk or lace frills covering the shoulders and low décolletage.
Bishop sleeve	Gathered sleeve falling full and gathered on to a band at the wrist.
Boa	Usually made of swansdown feathers or fur, a long tippet or scarf.
Boater	Stiff straw hat with a flat crown and narrow brim, surrounded by a petersham hatband.
Bolero	Short, loose-fitting jacket, usually sleeveless, and with the open fronts curved away.
Bollinger	Similar to a bowler hat with a knob on the round crown.
Bombazine	Usually black for mourning, a material in a twill effect made of silk and wool.
Bow tie	Necktie with a bow in front.
Bowler hat	Hard felt hat with domed crown and narrow rolled up brim.
Braces	Straps passing over the shoulders attached by buttons, front and back of trousers or breeches.
Bustle	Also known as a 'dress improver' or tournure pad or half

	hoop, worn at the back at waist height.
Calash	Large folding hood.
Capote	Soft crowned bonnet with a stiff brim.
Cape-paletot	Sleeved cloak with a deep cape.
Chatelaine	Ornamental chain from which hung various domestic items, such as scissors, button-hooks, thimble, needles, smelling salt containers.
Chemisette	Soft white material fill-in for a bodice.
Chignon	Hair arranged at the back of the head in loops or formal rows of curls, false hair often being used.
Clogs	Wooden soled shoes.
Coat sleeve	Cut in two pieces, straight and tubular with a slight curve at the elbow.
Corset	Undergarment with whalebone or steel ribs, worn to support the bosom and hold in the waist.
Covert coat	Short fly-fronted overcoat with side vents but without a central vent at the back.
Crêpe	Transparent and crimped gauze, usually in black.
Cravat	Neckcloth, often starched and covering the shirt front.
Crin	Stiffening.
Crinoline	Whalebone hoops joined by tapes or horsehair stiffened petticoat.
Crinolette	Half hooped crinoline.
Cross pockets	Pocket with a horizontal opening.
Curricle coat	Caped coat.
Dart	Pointed tuck of material sewn together to give a better fit.
Décolletage	Low neckline.
Deerstalker	Tweed cap with ear flaps which could be tied up over the crown or worn around the ears.
Dinner jacket	Worn informally with a roll collar and lapels to waist level and edged in silk or satin. The sleeves were cuffed.
Dolman	Mantle with the cape-like sleeves hanging loose.
Dress frock coat	Double-breasted frock coat with narrow silk-faced lapels and velvet collar, fastened low with two pairs of buttons.
Duster	Short summer coat worn also for motoring.
Engageantes	Tiered sleeve ruffles.
En Tablier	Decorative front pleated like an apron.
Falls	Buttoned front flap on trousers, breeches or pantaloons.
Fanchon	Lace trimming on kerchief worn over a cap, the ends trailing down the sides.
Ferronnière	Narrow metal or jewelled band worn around the head across the forehead.
Fly opening	Piece of material added at the edge of a garment to conceal the buttons.
Frock coat	Waisted and close fitting coat with collar, lapels and flapped hip pockets, buttoned only to the waist.

Gaiter	Ankle covering spreading over the top of a shoe with a strap holding it taut under the instep, usually buttoned on the outside.
Galoshes	Protective overshoes.
Garters	Strips of material, which could be elasticated, worn around the legs to keep the socks or stockings in place.
Garibaldi	Small-collared loose blouse worn with a waistbelt and usually trimmed with braid.
Gauging	Material gathered in parallel rows and sewn to give a honeycomb effect.
Gibus	Top hat with collapsible crown.
Gigot sleeve	Leg-of-mutton style sleeve, full at the shoulder becoming smaller to the elbows and tight at the wrists.
Gilet	Sleeveless blouse worn under a suit jacket as a fill-in.
Gore	Material cut in triangular pieces, the narrow parts to the top, to give a flared effect.
Habit shirt	Fill-in for a dress, also known as a chemisette.
Helmet hat	Hat with a helmet shaped crown and narrow brim.
Hessians	Short calf-length riding boots with a curve in the front and usually decorated with a tassel.
Highlows	Stout boots laced up in the front.
Homburg	Stiff felt hat with the brim slightly curved at the sides, the crown being indented from front to rear.
Jabot	Made-up type of cravat with frills of lace.
Jockey boots	Boots with turned-down tops.
Jockey cap	Hard, peaked cap.
Kilted	Overlapping pleats.
Knickerbockers	Loose breeches reaching just below the knees and gathered on to a band.
Lapels	Turned back upper part of a coat or jacket edge.
Lappets	Pendant streamers, often of lace hanging from headwear.
Lounge jacket	Short skirted jacket, slightly waisted, usually with rounded corners.
Medici collar	Usually of lace, standing up behind fan-wise.
Mentonnière	Goffered or gathered lace on bonnet strings forming a frill around lower part of face.
M-notch	Notch cut in shape of 'M' between the collar and coat lapel.
Mob-cap	Indoor cap with puffed crown and frilled border.
Mousquetaire cuff	Large turned-back cuff.
Mousquetaire hat	Brown mushroom-shaped straw hat, lace edging around brim.
Muffetees	Wrist muffs.
Muffin hat	Flat-crowned round hat with a narrow brim.
Norfolk jacket	Lounge jacket with box pleats front and back with patch pockets and belt of the same material. About 1894 a yoke was added from which the pleats emanated.

Opera hat	Hat with folding crown.
Oxfords or Oxonian shoes	High vamped lace-up shoes.
Page	Metal hook with ornamental head attached to waist with chain and clip suspended to hitch up the skirt.
Pagoda style	Sleeve cut wide to the elbow with inside seam caught at the bend and allowed to fall on outer side to wrist.
Paletot	Overcoat.
Paletot cloak	Short cloak with armhole slits.
Pantaloons	Close fitting tights.
Parasol	Ornamental umbrella.
Pardessus	Half or three-quarter length outdoor garment.
Pattens	Mainly worn in the country to raise the shoes from the road.
Pea jacket	Also known as a reefer or pilot coat, could be worn as a short jacket or coat, usually with large buttons.
Peg top sleeves	Similar to gigot sleeves.
Peg top trousers	Wide at waist, tightening towards the ankles.
Peignoir	Informal loose, unboned day attire.
Pelerine	Mantle-caped cloak with cape forming hanging sleeves.
Pelisse	Outdoor garment.
Pelisse-robe	Pelisse type day dress, fastening down the front.
Peplum	Short tunic or overskirt, shorter in front, falling in folds or flounces at the sides and back of skirt or bodice, attached to the waist.
Pilot coat	See pea jacket.
Plastron	Front panel of a skirt or bodice, usually in a contrasting colour.
Poke bonnet	Bonnet with the brim projecting forwards.
Polonaise	Overskirt, bunched up behind, revealing the underskirt.
Poncho	Large cape-like overgarment.
Pork pie hat	Flat and low crowned with narrow turned up brim.
Princess style	Bodice and skirt made in one without a waistseam, the skirt part being gored wider.
Puff	Gore of material in the back of the waistband of trousers, the sides having holes for laces to tighten waist as required.
Pumps	Thin soled shoes, usually worn in the evenings.
Raglan sleeve	Sleeve sewn in from underarm to neck without a shaped armhole, devised by Lord Raglan.
Reefer	See pea jacket, or it could be a thigh length top coat.
Revers	Turned back edge of a coat or jacket.
Roll collar	Turned over collar in one with the lapels.
Shawl collar	See roll collar.
Side edges	Scalloped flaps inserted into seams.
Side bodies	Separate panel inserted between underarm seams to give better fit.

Sortie-de-bal	Evening cloak with hood, usually of silk and with a quilted lining.
Spats	Similar to short gaiters and spatterdashes, buttoned down one side.
Spatterdashes	Type of leggings.
Stand collar	Collar without a turn-over.
Step	Gap between collar and lapel.
Stock	Stiffened neckcloth.
Sunray pleating	Pleated circular skirt.
Surtout	Overcoat.
Swallow tails	Tails of an evening dress coat.
Swiss belt	Waistband or belt, broadening in the front and back.
Tablier skirt	Sham apron denoted by trimmings on a skirt.
Taglioni	Short unwaisted overcoat usually trimmed with braid, named after Taglioni, an Italian dancer.
Tailor-made	Two piece costume made by tailors rather than dressmakers.
Talma	See poncho, long hooded cloak.
Tea gown	Similar to peignoir, worn informally in the afternoon.
Tibi	Loop fastening two buttons either side of an opening.
Top boots	Boots reaching just below knees with contrasting turn-over.
Top hat	Tall high-crowned hat.
Toque	Close fitting turban, brimless hat, made in a variety of materials including straw.
Tournure	See bustle.
Train	Back of a gown, longer and trailing the ground behind.
Trilby	Soft felt hat.
Turban	Material placed in folds around the head.
Ugly	Extra brim added to front of a bonnet, made with cane half hoops to fold back when not in use.
Ulster	Overcoat with either a whole or half belt.
Welt	Strengthened edge of a garment.
Zouave jacket	Similar to a bolero, but usually with sleeves.

Select Bibliography

Arnold, J., *Handbook of Costume*, Macmillan 1973;
 Patterns of Fashion (2 vols), Macmillan 1972
Asser, Joyce, *Historic Hairdressing*, Pitman 1966
Boehn, M. von, *Modes and Manners* (8 vols), Harrap 1926-35
Barfoot, A., *Everyday Costume in England*, Batsford 1966
Boucher, F., *History of Costume in the West*, Thames & Hudson 1967;
 20,000 Years of Fashion, Abrams
Bradfield, N., *Costume in Detail, Women's Dress 1730-1930*, Harrap;
 Historical Costumes of England, Harrap 1958
Brooke, Iris, *History of English Costume*, Methuen 1937;
 English Children's Costume; A. & C. Black 1965;